The Self-Destruction Handbook

THE

SELF-DESTRUCTION

Handbook

8 Simple Steps to an Unhealthier You

ADAM WASSON AND JESSICA STAMEN

THREE RIVERS PRESS • NEW YORK

Published by Three Rivers Press, New York, New York.
Member of the Crown Publishing Group, a division of Random House, Inc.
www.crownpublishing.com

THREE RIVERS PRESS and the Tugboat design are registered trademarks of Random House, Inc.

Printed in the United States of America
Design by Susan Hood

Library of Congress Cataloging-in-Publication Data
    Wasson, Adam.
      The self-destruction handbook: 8 simple steps to an unhealthier
    you / Adam Wasson & Jessica Stamen.—1st ed.
      1. Conduct of life—Humor.   2. Self-destructive behavior—
    Humor.   3. Health—Humor.   I. Stamen, Jessica.   II. Title.
    PN6231.C6142W37 2004
    818'.602—dc22   2003024499

    ISBN 1-4000-5033-2

10 9 8 7 6 5 4 3 2 1

First Edition

In memory of Owen Jenkins, who taught us that satire is the last refuge of the patriot.

Publisher's Disclaimer

THIS BOOK MAY BE HAZARDOUS IF READ WITHOUT IRONY.

Authors' Disclaimer

IF YOU CAUSE YOURSELF UNWANTED HARM BECAUSE OF
SOMETHING YOU READ IN THIS BOOK, THEN YOU ARE AN IDIOT.

Contents

Introduction

*C*ONGRATULATIONS! In picking up this book you have already accomplished more than you may realize. For one thing, you've made a statement about yourself—you are not someone who simply follows the crowd. Let's face it, there are thousands of books on how to avoid self-destructive behavior. As far as we know, however, this is the world's first book on how to embrace self-destruction, enjoy it, and pursue it to its fullest extent. Take a moment just to congratulate yourself on being unique enough to recognize this fact, and brave enough to investigate it.

The Self-Hurt Goal

Our goal here is simple: We want to help you not help yourself. To that end, we offer advice on everything from how to stalk an ex to how to smoke with emphysema. Wondering which gateway drug is right for you? This book will help you decide. Not sure how much degradation you can take? Probably more than you think: We'll help you push your limits.

No matter what self-destructive behavior you're interested in pursuing, chances are we've got some valuable advice and encouragement for you.

Destruction Isn't Death

Self-destruction is not suicide. In fact, they are very different. Suicidal people want to end life altogether, whereas self-destructives enjoy debasing themselves, degrading others, and generally wreaking physical and emotional havoc on the world around them. There is nothing more life-affirming than total destruction, whereas death, in our opinion, is zero fun.

If you are suicidal, then you have probably lost all sense of irony and should look elsewhere for help.

If, on the other hand, you hope to mastermind and botch multiple suicide attempts in order to frighten and manipulate people who care about you, we've got some real gems for you in chapter 8.

Your Self-Hurt Journey

We're not going to lie to you. Self-destruction can be a difficult and sometimes lonely road. That is why, if you remember only one thing as you read this book, we want you to remember this: The whole point of self-destruction is that it's fun. If you're not having fun, then you might as well be taking vitamins, "working" on your relationships, and reading self-help books.

Your goal here should be to develop and pursue your self-destructive tendencies to their fullest potential, and to have a good time doing it. Before you read further, we'd like you to reflect for a moment on the most self-destructive thing you've ever done. Gratifying, wasn't it?

Okay, let's get to it!

The Self-Destruction Handbook

1.

12 Steps to a Drinking "Problem"

Do You Have a Drinking Problem?

1. *What time do you normally begin drinking?*
   a. After work (5 POINTS)
   b. Noon or before (10 POINTS)
   c. No idea—pawned watch for beer money (15 POINTS)

2. *After a night of drinking, have you ever:*
   a. Awakened next to someone unattractive? (5 POINTS)
   b. Awakened next to someone you didn't recognize? (10 POINTS)
   c. Awakened next to Charlie Sheen? (25 POINTS)

3. *If pulled over and asked to walk a straight line, would you be most likely to:*
   a. Vomit? (5 POINTS)
   b. Walk a line that's straight if you look at it from "down here"? (10 POINTS)
   c. Offer the officer "one for the road"? (17 POINTS)

4. When your wife threatens to leave you, do you generally:

    a. Tell her to go ahead and git her fat butt on   (5 POINTS)
       outta the trailer?

    b. Contemplate over a fine cognac the   (10 POINTS)
       existential vagaries that have led to this
       particular nadir?

    c. Offer her "one for the road"?   (17 POINTS)

5. This question to be answered while drunk:

    a. a   (5 POINTS)
    b. b   (5 POINTS)
    c. Huh?   (10 POINTS)

SCORING THE QUIZ

If you had the motor skills and mental acuity to complete this quiz, then you do not have a truly serious drinking problem. Please read on, however. There is hope!

Step 1: Admit that You Do Not Have a Problem

The first thing that you *must* do, before you even consider embarking on the rest of our program, is admit that you do not have a problem. Of course you would like to have a problem. All creative, sexy, and artistic people possess powerful dark sides, and there is no more effective and time-tested way of expressing a dark side than through serious alcohol abuse.

 DID YOU KNOW? WINSTON CHURCHILL, ERNEST HEMINGWAY, AND JACKSON POLLOCK ALL HAD SERIOUS DRINKING PROBLEMS. RICHARD SIMMONS DOES NOT DRINK.

Developing a legitimate drinking problem can seem like an overwhelming task, and that is why it is so important that you approach the process one drink, one step, and one day at a time. If you can just summon up the strength to take this first step, and admit that you do not yet have a problem, we will be able to assist you the rest of the way.

Step 2: Make It a Double

A fundamental tenet of our program is that **you will always have help,** and one of the most important forms of help will come in the form of your **"alcohol sponsor"** or **"drinking buddy."** Your drinking buddy is the person who challenges you to do one more shot, the person who holds your hair out of the vomit when you throw up and pass out. Your drinking buddy makes sure that no "significant other" ever comes between you and your. In fact, you can and should think of your drinking buddy as your "insignificant other."

Who's Your Buddy?

Drinking buddies should be genial and, most important, constantly available. It is also recommended that your drinking buddy be substantially less attractive than you, though free of any obvious physical deformity that might hinder their effectiveness as your **"wingman."**

JARGON ALERT: A "wingman" is a friend whose presence allows you to engage two members of the opposite sex in conversation. It is important that your "wingman" seem attractive enough to encourage the other duo to come over, but not so attractive that you yourself are demoted to talking to the other team's lesser member.

The typical drinking buddy/wingman will possess a single unfortunate facial feature—a lazy eye, for instance, or disturbingly prominent gums. Those desiring a somewhat trendier "buddy" look may want to consider someone with a mild mental or neurological handicap. Neurologically challenged people can actually appear very attractive from a distance, and it is only once the conversation has commenced that your chosen interlocutors will notice something amiss. They will most likely assume that your friend is inebriated and/or a member of a fraternity. Even should they divine the truth, however, no remotely PC person will be able to withdraw from the conversation for at least several minutes, thus giving you a comfortable amount of time in which to make your move.

Step 3: Renounce God

Renouncing your belief in this Santa Claus–like figure is an essential part of your drinking journey, because it allows you to confront the horror of human existence without the anesthetizing influence of religious cliché. Once you understand and accept the **utter inefficacy of prayer,** you will be forced to find other ways to avoid actually working for what you want. This, of course, is where alcohol will come in.

Step 4: Find Your Role Model

Once you have renounced God, you may find yourself searching for some other sort of guidance. You can find it in your **drinking role model.** From Bacchus to Boris Yeltsin, inspirational icons have always been an important aspect of the sincere alcohol abuser's drinking journey. Some people will be fortunate enough to find inspiration **within their own family:** alcoholic stepfathers, rebellious "party girl" sisters, even a mother mired deep in a haze of bourbon-scented denial can all be excellent drinking role models. Those without such familial connections need not worry, however, because we have compiled a list of other possibilities for you. Go ahead and browse through them, and select the one who most nearly approximates the kind of drinker you'd like to be.

Role Models for Women

The Cosmo Girl

ROLE MODELS The *Sex and the City* girls, Holly Golightly, the Bush daughters.

DRINK OF CHOICE Apple martini, raspberry martini, chocolate martini, mango martini . . .

PRO You will feel like a movie star.

CON You probably won't look like one. After all those expensive sugary drinks you will be fat and poor in no time.

The Southern Belle

ROLE MODELS Any Tennessee Williams heroine, Steel Magnolia, or Ya-Ya sister.

DRINK OF CHOICE Mint juleps on the porch in summer, bourbon the rest of the time.

PRO You will have men wrapped around your finger and somehow look sexy despite being perpetually covered in sweat.

CON This type of drinker has traditionally found herself involved in incest, abuse, murder, and/or scenery-chewing.

The White Trash

ROLE MODELS Kelly Bundy, Pamela Anderson.

DRINK OF CHOICE Whatever the boys are buying, and make it a double.

PRO The drinks are cheap.

CON So are you.

Role Models for Men

The Smooth Operator

ROLE MODEL James Bond.
DRINK OF CHOICE Martini. Vodka martini.
PRO Attract the attention of beautiful women who speak several languages, know martial arts, and have double entendres for names.
CON They're only paying attention to you because they assume you are gay and, thus, pose no threat.

The Literary Legend

ROLE MODELS Hemingway, Fitzgerald, Faulkner.
DRINK OF CHOICE The hard stuff.
PRO You'll be the toast of the literary community.
CON No one reads books anymore. The literary community consists of you, a pen, and an empty bottle.

The Party Animal

ROLE MODELS Belushi brothers, Baldwin brothers, fraternity brothers.
DRINK OF CHOICE Beer. Preferably overfoamed from an ineptly tapped keg.
PRO You are sure to be the life of the party.
CON Once you graduate and your friends get jobs and wives, it will be a party of one.

Step 5: Make Drinking Fun—
Drinking Games to Play Alone

Though drinking games are often associated with college fra-
ternities and sororities, there is no reason anyone, no matter
how unpopular and lonely, should deny themselves the pleasure of these activities. Like any other all-consuming pursuit,
drinking can sometimes seem like hard work—especially
when you are alone. In such instances, the right game at the
right time can lift your spirits and remind you how much fun
"problem" drinking can be.

QUARTERS Stand outside a liquor store with a crudely scrawled
VETERAN sign around your neck and a battered Styrofoam
cup in your hand. While staring into the distance with a look
of abject desperation, politely ask passersby if they can "help
you out" with a quarter. If anyone asks what specifically you
are a veteran of, simply say, "Hard times, brother. Hard times."

TV DRINKING GAME Watch a classic TV sitcom, such as *Leave
It to Beaver*. Drink each time you see an instance of moral rec-
titude, parental affection, or any other "family value" that you
yourself were denied as a child.

NUMBERS Known also as "drunk dialing," Numbers is a game
in which you dial the phone number of someone you have a
crush on but whom you have never been able to tell for fear of
rejection. Whether you reach them or their answering
machine, make sure to begin and end the conversation with
"I'm so drunk," as in, "Hi, Brad? Oh my God, I'm so drunk.
This is Jennifer, Jennifer Saveri, and you probably don't know

me very well but I think you're just so . . . so beautiful, and
smart, and I know people think I'm a dork but I really think I
could . . . or we could, you know . . . oh my God, I'm so drunk."

Step 6: Begin to Stage
Inappropriate Outbursts

First of all, congratulations! This is Step 6, and that means
that you are already at the halfway point in our program. Give
yourself a big pat on the back for that. Now that you're
halfway through, it is time to start taking your drinking public, and there is no better way to debut your problem than
with a wholly inappropriate public outburst.

The main considerations in staging an inappropriate outburst are **venue** and **audience.** Venue is particularly important: A tantrum in a dive bar around a bunch of other drunks
might go largely unnoticed, but the same tantrum at a PTA
meeting would be far more inappropriate and, thus, effective.

You should also try to decide before the event what
response you want to provoke from your audience. Ideally,
your behavior will garner stares of disapproval and a murmur
of general embarrassment, but stop short of provoking physical intervention by civic authorities.

The "Rite" Site

The best combinations of inappropriate venue and impres-
sionable audience tend to occur at large gatherings of family
and friends, especially those centered around religious rites
or rituals.

Weddings, of course, offer the ideal blend of venue and
audience, and the procedure for an inappropriate wedding

outburst can serve as a model for other outbursts. After becoming inebriated at the wedding reception of a close friend or relative, break down in tears and proclaim loudly that no one will ever really love you. When the newly married bride or groom tries to comfort you, vomit.

Other events to consider are **funerals, anniversaries,** and **Christmas Eve vespers.**

NOTE Inappropriate outbursts do not necessarily have to be full-blown tantrums. Timing and content are just as important as intensity and duration. Even a single word can be effective if properly delivered. A shouted, slightly slurred "Freebird" at your niece's next choral recital, for instance, can speak volumes, as can a wincing "Yee-ouch" at a briss.

Step 7: Reveal Bare Breasts and/or Buttocks when Drunk

Perhaps no physical activity is as strongly associated with copious drinking as "the flash." Men should always attempt to flash when women are present, as the sight of a man's bare hindquarters provokes a primal, hormonal response from any female of reproductive age. Women should make sure, whenever possible, to flash in front of the *Girls Gone Wild* video cameras. There is an excellent chance that this will eventually make you a star.

The BT (aka "Bare Tits")

Flashing breasts is almost always a good idea, and when engaging in a BT there is really only one question to answer: top up or top down?

TOP UP If wearing a T-shirt, then pulling the top up is obviously your only choice. The top-up is a perfectly legitimate and time-tested flashing maneuver, but it does suggest a certain amount of insincerity, as it allows you simply to lower it back down at any second.

TOP DOWN Pulling the top down is a courageous move that works well with halter tops, tube tops, or any kind of bikini top. There is something extremely alluring about a woman with her top pulled down, clinging just above the hips, something so suggestive of a wanton tussle in the closet, a ravishing tryst in the boudoir, a rapacious interlude in the back of a Jeep Cherokee. It's really quite enchanting. We highly recommend the top-down option.

NOTE TO MEN Unless you are at the beach, playing strip poker, or Italian, keep your shirt on.

The BA (aka "Bare Ass")

When it comes to flashing your nether regions, it is easiest simply to think of your options in terms of the lunar cycle.

The half moon

The full moon

The waxing moon

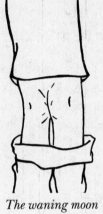

The waning moon

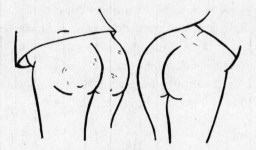

The honeymoon

The bitter moon

Step 8: Engage in an Inappropriate and Degrading Alcohol-Related Sexual Encounter

The inappropriate and degrading sexual encounter is an essential ingredient in your alcoholic cocktail. If you pick the right person, time, and place, just a small investment of time and energy can have repercussions that last for decades.

Who

Encounters usually involve one of the following partners: a coworker, a neighbor, a friend of your parents, or an ex. If none of these is available or interested, potential secondary targets might include your doorman, the parking garage attendant at work, or even the bus driver. The most important thing is that the person be someone you cannot avoid seeing repeatedly in the future, and that each meeting will inevitably make both of you **excruciatingly uncomfortable.**

When

Degrading encounters generally take place toward the end of a stressful workweek, during holiday parties, and/or following a particularly brutal breakup.

Where

Location is not as important as choice of partner, but the most popular choices include a desk in the boss's office, an unlocked copy room or broom closet, a second cousin's child-hood bedroom, or the backseat of a 1996 Ford Taurus.

How

There is not a great deal of documentation on how to initiate the encounter, because the participants rarely remember how it happened. One thing that is known, however, is that sometime prior to the encounter each participant should discuss the other person with a close friend and say, "I would never, *ever* go there."

 DID YOU KNOW? *IN 18 PERCENT OF ABORTED SEXUAL ENCOUNTERS, COMPLETION WAS NOT ATTAINED BECAUSE THE MAN WAS "TOO DRUNK." THIRTY-SEVEN PERCENT WERE ABORTED BECAUSE THE WOMAN WAS "NOT DRUNK ENOUGH."*

Step 9: Take Revenge for the Problems Others Have Caused You

As you move into the final stages of the program, it is important that you begin to blame others for your problems and attempt to revenge yourself upon them. This revenge might be as simple as a bitch-slap to the face of a shrewish sibling, or as complex as seducing your ex's best friend. The kind of revenge you choose will of course be specific to your individual tastes, but in order to provide you with some sense of direction we have listed a few of the most common and effective types of revenge.

THE INSULT When wreaking verbal revenge, try to avoid discussing things in terms of your feelings, e.g., "I felt really deserted when you left me." Opt instead for direct declarative statements, such as "No one will ever love you, you whore."

SELF-ABUSE Self-abuse is particularly effective with parents and/or ex-girlfriends with a self-abnegation or "martyr" complex. Try punching a wall or wrecking your car in a drunken fit. Assuming the person still loves you, they will be racked with guilt and visit you repeatedly in the hospital, where you can press the revenge home with various versions of the insult (see above). One risk of the self-abuse method is that your chosen target may not actually love you and will express only disinterest and/or amusement at hearing of your accident.

URINATION Few things are as satisfying or truly expressive of disdain as the simple physical act of urination. It is generally most effective to urinate on something of symbolic value, such as an ex-boyfriend's car or an ex-girlfriend's cat. Whether your target is a Celica or a Siamese, though, the most important thing is to be well hydrated. There is little more disheartening than whipping it out for a savage torrent and achieving only a genial trickle.

Step 10: Find Your Enabler

As your erratic behavior begins to alienate those close to you, it is important that you cultivate a relationship with someone who will care for you no matter how low you sink, someone you will be able to use and manipulate even while barely conscious. This person is your **enabler.**

Strong yet docile, enablers are like **gentle herd beasts** on the great plain of life. Though not especially colorful or exciting creatures, they are nonetheless necessary to maintaining a delicately balanced dysfunctional ecosystem.

Enabler Wrangling

Enabler wrangling is a delicate skill, and you must understand the bovine nature of your enabler if you are going to milk the situation for all it's worth. Enablers value themselves primarily in terms of their ability to nurture and benefit others, and the more you are able to undermine their confidence, the more they will seek to bolster their self-esteem by being a good nurturer to you.

It may seem counterintuitive that someone would be nice to you because you are cruel to them, but this is the way of enablers. Phrases such as "Gaining a little weight there?" and "Can't you do anything right?" can be extremely useful in prodding your enabler to do your bidding. Indeed, the beauty of a true enabler is that the more uncivil you become, the more they want to "be there" for you. It is almost too easy. Of course, this is assuming that you are able to find yourself a genuine enabler, and therein lies the rub. The difficult thing is not so much cultivating a good enabler once you've found them, but tracking down and corralling them in the first place.

The best enablers generally come from hearty and reliable enabler stock, and a family history of enabling is perhaps the best indicator that they will instinctually be both caretaking and docile. Often, however, you do not know your current or prospective enabler's lineage, and in this case the best way to assess their enabler potential is through our thorough **five-point inspection.**

The Enabler Inspection

PHYSICAL "ROBUSTNESS" Enablers should typically be 20 to 40 pounds overweight. Overweight people are both jolly and trustworthy, and capable of bearing heavy loads. They are also unlikely to have other romantic offers.

NAME TAG A name tag, especially when pinned to a uniform of any kind, signifies both steady employment and lack of ambition—both of which are essential qualities in a potential enabler.

BOUNTIFUL MAMMARIES In a woman, large, drooping breasts signify maternal, caretaking instincts. In a man, they signify an absence of testosterone and pride.

GOOD TEETH Good, strong teeth indicate both responsibility and hygiene.

A RED SOX BASEBALL CAP Anyone willing to support a losing team year after seemingly endless year has both the stamina and the delusional optimism of a dependable enabler.

ECOUTEZ, ENABLER

If you are blind and cannot conduct a visual inspection, listen for these key phrases in order to identify, and measure your progress with, a potential enabler.

- A person who refers to children as **"our most precious resource"** quite likely possesses both the weak mind and the soft heart of a good enabler.

- The phrase **"My lord and savior Jesus Christ"** is an excellent indicator of enabler potential, as it suggests that the speaker possesses a capacity for self-delusion combined with a chronic "follower" or "flock" mentality.

- The phrase **"Fuck me"** is another excellent indicator of enabler potential. Generally uttered prior to or during sexual intercourse, this exclamation suggests not merely a willingness but indeed an eagerness to be used and abused in the service of your needs.

- The phrase **"No hablo inglés"** suggests that the speaker takes an unconditionally supportive approach to committed relationships.

- The ultimate enabler phrase remains, of course, **"I love you."** This is the verbal equivalent of baring one's neck to an oncoming predator, a shorthand way of abdicating the primal struggle for supremacy and acknowledging lifetime servitude.

Step 11: One Day at a Time

Now that you have mastered the basic techniques of binge drinking and have your support team firmly in place, you are ready to make your final leap to the problem drinker's ultimate test: a **bender.**

JARGON ALERT: A *bender* **is a drinking binge that lasts for 24 hours or more. Its name comes from the fact that such prolonged drinking generally results in periodic bouts of nausea and cramping, causing the drinker's torso to bend and/or convulse.**

Like a marathon to a distance runner, the bender is the purest test of a drinker's will and commitment. It takes enormous dedication and intense training, and only the strongest survive. F. Scott Fitzgerald, it is rumored, routinely went on three-day benders, and Hemingway is said to have achieved benders lasting as long as two weeks. At this point, of course, a two-week drinking binge may seem like an impossible goal, but if you take it one day at a time and stick to our training plan, you will soon be using up "sick days" like there is no tomorrow.

The Warm-Up

It is important to get yourself warmed up and in shape before embarking on a serious bender.

GARGLING Gargling with Listerine will open up the throat, and will also habituate your larynx to the burning sensation characteristic of hard alcohol.

DRY HEAVES A few half-speed lurching or retching motions, also known as **dry heaves,** will ensure that you don't pull any muscles when it actually comes time for a convulsive projectile vomit.

THE FLOP It is a good idea to practice allowing your body to relax when you fall. One way to do this is to engage in a "trust exercise" with your drinking buddy. As your buddy falls backward toward you, relaxed and trusting, simply step back and allow them to crash to the floor. Because of their relaxed posture, it is doubtful that they will suffer more than minor injuries, and you will gain valuable experience by watching them fall in this relaxed state.

Training

While wearing sweats and a headband, sit on your couch with a bottle of vodka and listen to "Eye of the Tiger."

Leave for Las Vegas

Once you are ready to attempt your first bender, drive or fly to Las Vegas. The trademark Vegas combination of bounteous free liquor and soul-deadening capitalistic excess provides the perfect bender cocktail. This unique combination has inspired self-destructive benders in celebrities ranging from Dean Martin and Frank Sinatra to Dennis Rodman and Ben Affleck. Wayne Newton has apparently been sustaining a Las Vegas bender since 1972.

DID YOU KNOW? THE ANCIENT HEBREW WORD FOR "DEATH" IS THE SAME AS THE WORD FOR "BLACKOUT." THIS HAS LED SOME MIDRASHIC SCHOLARS TO SPECULATE THAT JESUS' SUPPOSED "RESURRECTION" WAS NOT IN FACT A RISING FROM DEATH, BUT RATHER A BRUTAL MORNING-AFTER ON THE HEELS OF A THREE-DAY BENDER.

Step 12: Rehab

Most true benders eventually come to an end in some sort of alcohol rehabilitation facility. You can and should think of rehab as a party thrown to celebrate your success. If you are called on to make a speech, remember to thank those who made your drinking problem possible.

Like any gathering of like-minded individuals, rehab can be an excellent place to share and acquire technical knowledge. From revenge techniques to hangover cures, your fellow attendees have a wealth of inebriation experience, and you should avail yourself of it as much as possible.

Congratulations!

Making it to rehab was your final step—can you believe how fast it all went? In addition to our heartfelt felicitations, we would like to leave you with one final promise: Our program will always be there for you. No matter how many relationships you shatter, no matter how many jobs you lose or cars you wreck, these 12 steps will never desert you—even when everyone else does. Cheers!

2.

Why Smoking Is Cool

Are You Cool Enough to Smoke?

1. *Approximately how many days per week do you sit on an open range wearing chaps and a Stetson?*
   a. 1–2   (10 POINTS)
   b. Whenever the do-gies are rollin'   (15 POINTS)
   c. When you're feeling "kitschy"   (3 POINTS)

2. *As a woman, you would smoke in order to indicate:*
   a. Moral flexibility   (5 POINTS)
   b. Oral flexibility   (10 POINTS)
   c. Both A and B, plus a certain Bette Davis–like *je ne sais quoi*   (25 POINTS)

3. *The coolest place to put out a cigarette is:*
   a. On the heel of your shoe   (2 POINTS)
   b. On a windswept yacht among windswept friends with windswept yet full-bodied hair   (10 POINTS)
   c. On the exposed forearm of a grimacing henchman   (25 POINTS)

4. *If an attractive European woman asked you for a light, you would most likely:*

   a. Search through your all-purpose fanny pack (0 POINTS) for a small emergency flashlight

   b. Strike a match and cup your strong hands (10 POINTS) gently, tenderly, shielding her cigarette from the elements as she leans suggestively into the flame

   c. Say "my pleasure" in a faux British accent (10 POINTS) while flipping open your gold-plated lighter in a way that draws subtle attention to the Rolex on your wrist

5. *When you dream of Joe Camel, you generally find these dreams to be:*

   a. Mildly erotic (5 POINTS)

   b. Disturbingly erotic (5 POINTS)

   c. More accurately described as erotic (5 POINTS) prophecies than dreams

SCORING THE QUIZ

No matter how many points you score, you are cool enough to smoke. Why? Because smoking can *make* you cool, even if you are not cool already. Of course, not everyone can be Marlon Brando just because they have a Lucky Strike in their mouth, but you will definitely be cooler than you are now.

Why Smoking Is Cool

From Sir Walter Raleigh to Kurt Cobain, the world's coolest people have always been smokers. Smoking is sexy, rebellious, and a fantastic way to meet Europeans.

DID YOU KNOW? SEVENTY PERCENT OF SUPERMODELS CONSIDER THEMSELVES "DEDICATED SMOKERS."

Let's not kid ourselves, however. Learning to smoke is hard. If it were easy, everyone would be doing it. Even more difficult than learning to smoke is maintaining your habit once you have acquired it. Every day, thousands of people give in to social pressure and give up the sexiness and individuality symbolized by their cigarettes. You don't want to be a quitter, do you? Assuming you don't, you should keep **two goals** in mind while you read this chapter: First, we need to **get you started** smoking. Second, and just as important, we want to make sure that you **look and feel cool while smoking,** so that you will never be tempted to abandon the habit.

SMOKY SAYS: EIGHTY PERCENT OF SMOKERS DIE BEFORE THE AGE OF 75. EIGHTY PERCENT OF PEOPLE OVER THE AGE OF 75 ROUTINELY SAY, "I WISH I WERE DEAD."

Getting Started

The starting method we recommend is to work into your habit gradually, taking advantage of a large number of products that can help your body adjust to nicotine even before you begin inhaling it on a regular basis. Feel free to sample any or all of the products below in order to find which ones work best for you, and use them to ease yourself methodically into your nicotine craving.

NICORETTE GUM Nicotine-laden gum is a tasty and effective way to begin acquiring a nicotine habit. You are probably already used to chewing bubble gum, so this will hardly be any adjustment at all.

THE PATCH The nicotine patch can be an excellent cigarette "warm-up." While most people simply stick these patches on their arms, there are also many more creative places to "patch one on." A patch on the extreme lower back can be an excellent accent to low-rider jeans, for example, and the eye-"patch" has recently come back into fashion for the first time since Spanish galleons sailed the high seas.

CHEW If you are a young male from any rural state south of Ohio, chewing tobacco is a perfectly acceptable way to begin.

LOW-TAR There is nothing wrong with low-tar cigarettes. We all have to crawl before we can walk, and it is okay to start out mild before you get wild. If you are a man, however, please try not to do it when you are in public.

LIGHTING YOUR FIRE
....

The light is the single most overlooked aspect of smoking cool. Without fire, after all, there's no smoke.

THE MATCH Use a match only if you are confident and have steady hands. There is nothing less cool than multiple strikes, or lighting up and having the match go out. This puts a serious amount of pressure on the next match. Should the second match also go out, you might as well leave, because you are essentially castrated in that venue.

THE DISPOSABLE Perfectly acceptable if you are home-less, camping, or a resident of a third-world country. Helpful hint: Make sure the child lock is off.

THE ZIPPO Proper Zippo technique requires a smooth, well-practiced coordination of fingers, wrist, and palm into a precisely timed spasm, or "jerk." Teenaged boys between the ages of 13 and 15 are for some reason par-ticularly adept with the Zippo, as are single men who work in the tech industry.

THE TORCH Flameless "torches" are the sports cars of lighters. Sleek, sophisticated, and powerful, a gold- or nickel-plated flameless says "I have a small penis" for about $98,700 less than a Porsche.

THE TRICK LIGHT Unless you are in Vegas, avoid any form of the trick light. If the trick works, you look like a cheesy operator who is trying too hard. If it doesn't, there is a good possibility that you will set either yourself or some-one else on fire.
....

Smoking with Style

Once you have accustomed your body to nicotine and are ready to start smoking, it is important to learn solid fundamentals. The best way to do this is to imitate and practice an established technique before striking out on your own. There are a variety of classic smoking styles for you to choose from, and we have listed some of the most popular below, complete with instructive illustrations. Make sure to choose a style you feel comfortable with, because if all goes well it will be with you until the end.

THE BOGART Hold cigarette between your thumb and first two fingers. Bring it to and from the mouth in a masculine, direct line, without unnecessary flourishes.

Note: This technique looks particularly cool if your head is almost grotesquely oversized in comparison with your neck and shoulders.

THE NAZI Hold cigarette between index and middle fingers, cupping fingers slightly toward your mouth. Bring it to and from the mouth in short, staccato bursts. The lips should curl slightly and anti-Semitically upward on the exhale.

THE BRANDO The secret to the Brando is to completely avoid touching the cigarette with your hands. Take it directly from the pack to the mouth, and then leave it hanging from the lower lip. Inhale as necessary.

THE MUSHMOUTH Before taking a drag off of someone else's cigarette, allow saliva to accumulate between your lips and gums. Take a lengthy inhale and roll the cigarette slightly in your mouth until the filter is fully saturated. Then hand it back.

THE STEM FATALE In the shadows the tip of her cigarette flamed once and went dark, like a little sun dropping off the edge of the world. Except the sun never went down that fast. But this woman, well, she always went down fast and came up faster. A thin ring of gray hung around her like a halo, and as soon as I saw it I knew what was coming. Where there's smoke, there's fire.

THE DIE-HARD: SMOKING WITH EMPHYSEMA Ask a relative who's angling for an inheritance to smuggle cigarettes into your hospital room. Request that they light the cigarette for you (without Mushmouthing if possible), and gently insert it into your tracheotomy hole.

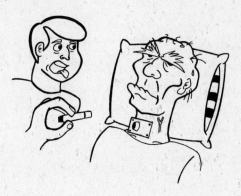

BRANDED

You are what you smoke. Here is what your brand of cigarette says about you:

KOOL You're slick, suave, and sophisticated. Clad in leather and accompanied by a smooth blaxploitation bass line, you always know what side of the street you're standing on: the Kool side.

LUCKY STRIKE You are indeed lucky. With a deluxe trailer and a full, shiny mullet, you embody a kind of post-pastoral chic. Relax and enjoy that smoke—your lottery ticket should be coming through any time now.

PARLIAMENT You are either a member of the British aristocracy or a direct descendant thereof. Ashtray, milord?

AMERICAN SPIRIT It is clear you have profited off the local casinos, since you are able to afford brand-name cigarettes, unlike so many in your tribe who blow their paltry salaries on hooch and must craft their cigarettes from animal skins and soot.

CAMEL Sadly, you have fallen prey to a terrorist plot to beguile Americans into worshipping the camel, the very animal that enabled the rise of the desert people. Do not be fooled by the kindly "Joe Camel"—he is in reality "Youssef bin Camel," and he's sneaky.

Waiting to Exhale

An essential yet overlooked aspect of smoking technique is the exhale, or **finish.** Like a dismount in gymnastics, the exhale can ultimately make or break your performance.

Nostril Exhale

DIFFICULTY Very difficult
COOLNESS FACTOR High
The nostril exhale is one of a genre of difficult moves that also includes the "exhale while talking." The key to all such moves is that they be accomplished naturally, as though without effort or planning. Devotees of rhinoplasty should beware, however, because nothing announces "nose-job" like a single-nostril exhale.

The In-Your-Face

DIFFICULTY Difficulty is low, but danger factor is high
COOLNESS FACTOR Depends who's being exhaled upon.
Imagine Humphrey Bogart exhaling on Peter Lorre. This is a daring and impressive exhale, but you had better be prepared to back it up.

The Thought Bubble

DIFFICULTY Low
COOLNESS FACTOR Depends on whether or not you're in a coffee shop.
A straight-up exhale that is considerate of others and gives the exhaler a contemplative, artistic appearance.

The Smoke-Ring

DIFFICULTY High
COOLNESS FACTOR Depends on whether or not you are over 16. Not a particularly attractive exhale, the smoke ring should generally be confined to the genre of cute party tricks.

The Pretender

We've all seen them. That one feeb at the party who likes to be seen with a cigarette but never inhales. This facade cannot be hidden on the exhale. Telltale signs are eye-twitching and tearing as the mouthful of uninhaled smoke drifts directly upward after the faux exhale. Pretenders should be avoided and ostracized at all times.

The Lung-Wracking Cough

Longtime smokers will often accompany their exhale with a deathly, tubercular rattle or a half-smothered wheeze. While obviously not attractive in and of itself, this exhale does announce a longstanding dedication to smoking, and garners respect from serious smokers in much the same way that the Parkinson's-ridden Muhammad Ali garners applause and admiration from boxing fans.

Smokabulary

Like most activities, smoking has certain terms and phrases that only the cognoscenti know. Because smoking is very sexy, the meaning of such terms often changes depending on the speaker's gender and physical attractiveness.

When a Smoker Says, "Do You Mind if I Smoke?"

SHE MEANS "I am going to smoke whether you like it or not, but this way I have your attention before I reach delicately into the pack, slowly pull out a long cylindrical object, and sensuously insert it into my mouth."

HE MEANS "I'm a poser who is only smoking to impress you."

When a Smoker Says, "Do You Have a Light?"

SHE MEANS "You seem nonthreatening. May I borrow a lighting implement?"

HE MEANS "I actually have a light of my own, but I am confident that this seemingly benign question will pave the way to a torrid sexual encounter."

When a Smoker Says, "I'm Going Outside for a Smoke"

SHE MEANS "There is a full drink in my hand and an epic line for the bathroom, so this is the only excuse I can muster to remove myself from this excruciating conversation."

HE MEANS "I am hoping you are also a smoker so I can get you outside and have four full minutes to make awkward and uninvited advances."

When a Smoker Says, "Can I Bum a Smoke?"

SHE MEANS "I am demonstrating my willingness to put something of yours into my mouth, so you can go ahead and bank on that BJ."

HE MEANS "I am poor and quite possibly homeless. Want to have sex?"

"MUST-SMOKE" SITUATIONS
....

After mind-blowing sex

Aboard any European airliner

After marginal sex

When under interrogation by authorities

During any conversation in which the word
   "deconstruction" is used

After bad sex

While standing on a breezy veranda surrounded by tall,
   elegant, sophisticated women whose open packs of
   Virginia Slims are all strategically placed toward the
   camera's vanishing point

Immediately prior to execution by firing squad
....

3

Your Brain on Drugs

What Should You Do?

1. *If a strange man tells you he's holding some "primo shit," he is most likely:*
   a. A Latino waste-management supervisor
   b. A drug dealer
   c. Your incontinent uncle

2. *If a strange man offers to sell you some "primo shit," you should:*
   a. Inform your parents that there is a drug dealer in the neighborhood
   b. Inform your friends that you know where to find some primo shit, then mark the price up a minimum of 50 percent
   c. Give your uncle a hard stare and say, "Primo, huh? I'll be the judge of that"

3. *If you see some of your classmates making a bong in shop class, you should:*
   a. Immediately inform the teacher, for your classmates' own good

b. Immediately kick your own ass to save your classmates the trouble

c. Remind your classmates that the "carb" needs to be above water-level

4. *If you enter the bathroom at a party and see a half-conscious girl convulsing on the floor, you should:*
   a. Get yourself a taste of that before she stops twitching
   b. Take a few fantasy pictures
   c. A and B, followed by immediate departure, because this party is headed for coptown

5. *If your date offers you drugs for cash, you should:*
   a. Ask him to take you home immediately
   b. Ask him to take you home immediately so you can grab some cash
   c. Tell him you have no money, but raise an eyebrow in order to suggest some "sweetness" in payment

SCORING THE QUIZ

We don't need to keep score, man. It's all about sharing the love.

Just Say "Know"

It is never too early to begin educating **both ourselves and our children** about drugs. The more we communicate to young people in a frank and open manner about drugs and their effects, the more likely it is they will be able to avoid the dangers that worry parents, from OD-ing to overpaying for inferior product. Too often, however, adults find that they themselves lack adequate information, and quite rightly wonder how they are supposed to teach their children something they actually know little about. The goal of this chapter is to remedy that **information deficit** and educate both parents and children about drugs and drug use. To that end, we have provided workshops geared to all developmental stages—from elementary, to junior high, to high school—and we encourage people of all ages to start at the beginning and work their way through. Even if the opening stages seem a bit too "elementary" for you, remember that it never hurts to review!

Elementary

Commonly Asked Questions

The best way to learn any new subject is by asking questions, so we're going to start out simply by answering some of the most common questions kids ask about drugs.

WHAT IS A DRUG?

A drug is something that you put in your body in order to feel different. It could be anything from aspirin or cold medicine to "harder" drugs like alcohol, marijuana, cocaine, heroin, X, G, super K, flake, skag, microdot, or croak.

HOW COME SOME DRUGS ARE OKAY AND OTHERS ARE BAD?

Generally, if wealthy white people use a drug, then it is legal. If Mexican or black people use it, then it is illegal and bad.

IS IT BETTER TO USE A BUTANE TORCH OR AN OXYACETYLENE TORCH WHEN FREEBASING?

Butane, because it provides a cleaner burn and you do not need the extra heat generated by the oxyacetylene mix.

Learning Your ABCs

When it comes to drugs, "ABC" stands for "All 'Bout Connections." This means that you need to understand who is who in the drug world before you even consider entering it yourself. You recognize the mailman because of the uniform he wears, right? Well, it is also important that you begin to recognize the delivery people and other "neighbors" in the drug community. The pictures on the following page will help you to practice your ABCs.

Can you find the **dealer** in this picture?

Can you find the **crack whore**?

Can you find the **narc**?

FUN WORD SEARCH

You can find the answers at the end of this chapter.

A	F	R	I	C	A	N	G	A	N	J	A	F	Q	S	R
L	S	Q	E	B	O	N	G	C	A	N	N	A	B	I	S
I	U	S	P	E	T	E	X	A	S	T	E	A	G	M	J
C	G	T	A	O	F	R	Y	R	T	A	E	H	W	K	W
E	A	D	O	S	W	E	S	W	E	E	T	L	U	C	Y
B	R	J	Y	K	S	J	R	K	S	E	L	S	E	E	W
T	W	S	H	F	E	I	B	O	O	D	T	J	R	F	A
O	E	E	O	F	N	C	N	U	U	N	U	B	O	N	C
K	E	N	S	I	X	E	S	O	U	M	A	W	A	S	K
L	D	A	K	L	M	B	Y	L	F	B	Y	I	C	C	Y
A	T	J	V	P	U	R	B	B	E	Y	N	S	H	K	W
S	I	Y	R	S	K	U	N	K	D	N	O	U	B	H	E
X	S	R	H	N	I	A	R	E	L	P	R	U	P	U	E
S	G	A	B	E	M	I	D	O	P	E	I	D	T	U	D
C	U	M	O	N	T	E	E	E	I	A	B	E	E	H	C
V	E	N	I	R	A	M	B	U	S	W	O	L	L	E	Y

African Ganja	Doobie	Sugarweed
Assassin of Youth	Dope	Sweet Lucy
Alice B. Toklas	Mary Jane	Texas Tea
Blunt	Monte	Toke
Bong	Purple Rain	Wacky Weed
Bud	Righteous Bush	Wheat
Cannabis	Roach	Yellow Subma-
Cheeba	Skunk	rine
Dime Bag	Spliff	Yerba

Junior High

The Placement Test

The following placement test will help to determine what "track" you should be on as you enter the next phase of your education. Once we know your track, we can begin funneling you toward the starter, or **"gateway,"** drugs appropriate to your temperament, ability, and tolerance level.

In which school-sponsored extracurricular activities do you plan to participate?
  a. Latin club, French club, Future Leaders of America, debate team, 4-H, lacrosse, field hockey, horseback riding, and/or others
  b. Does doodling count?
  c. School-sponsored activities are gay

If you answered "A" you are most likely an overachiever, which places you in the "uppers" track. The drugs you will eventually use are stimulants and mood elevators such as cocaine and crystal meth. Your gateway drugs, meanwhile, will be caffeine and Ritalin. You can find caffeine in many everyday products such as chocolate, Mountain Dew, and coffee. Consume as many of these as possible. As for Ritalin, the best place to find it is in the bookbags of your schoolmates with ADD. Simply remove a tablet and crush it up thoroughly on a flat surface such as your desk. Then, snort the crushed powder through a hollow cylindrical object, such as a rolled-up $100 bill.

If you answered "B" you are probably an artistic, dreamy type, which puts you into the "hallucinogens" track. The drugs that you will eventually experiment with are mind-expanding substances such as peyote, LSD, and "magic" mushrooms. While there are no exact gateway drugs for the hallucinogen track, it is nonetheless important to begin preparing your brain for bizarre and disturbing experiences by watching shows such as Disney's *Fantasia* and CNN's *Hannity and Colmes.*

If you answered "C," you may already have been labeled a hyperactive or "problem" student by your teachers, which suggests that you are an excellent candidate for self-medication with drugs from the "downers" track. Your ultimate goal on this track is *heroin,* but in the meantime you can jump right in with a classic and well-respected gateway drug: marijuana.

MARIJUANA PARTY ETIQUETTE
....

When rolling a joint at a party, try to do it as slowly and ostentatiously as possible. Make sure that everyone knows you are the joint master, and that the smoothness of their impending high will be almost entirely due to the excruciating exactitude of your studied technique.

When someone else is rolling a joint at a party, beg them to hurry the hell up.

If you are the girl who took one little faux inhale and then coughed, make sure to say, "Oh my God, you guys, I am so stoned." Doggedly repeat this phrase until people believe it.

....

Role-Playing

It is very important for parents and young people to communicate about drugs, and one excellent way to facilitate this is to engage in some role-playing exercises. Try to think of scenarios that parents and children can act out together, after which the whole family will discuss the choices you've made.

You might, for instance, have your father play the role of an **arresting officer.** What can you do to avoid arrest when you've clearly been caught "holding"? What would your mother do in the same situation? Can you use the fact that he's a male cop to your advantage?

Another scenario might take place at the airport, with your mother in the role of a Mexican security guard who has just discovered smuggled drugs inside your rectum. Is there any way out of this situation? Could you argue that the drugs are some sort of homeopathic suppository? How about a bribe? How much do you think it would take?

Drug Charades

Another excellent family role-playing game is **drug charades.** The game is played exactly like normal charades, where someone has to act out a person, place, or thing, except that you add the element of substance abuse as well. A participant might, for instance, have to act out "Isaac the Bartender from *Love Boat* on Heroin," or "Nancy Reagan Doing Ecstasy." This is a highly enjoyable game that can be very helpful in familiarizing you with the effects of various drugs even before you actually begin taking them.

PEER PRESSURE
....

People sometimes talk about pressure as if it were a bad thing, but it is not. If you were to cut yourself, for example, and no one applied pressure to the wound, you would soon bleed to death. Peer pressure is not unlike applying a tourniquet to the hemorrhaging social lives of your terminally uncool friends.

People often try to pressure their friends by telling them drugs will make them cool or help them fit in, but this is rarely effective. We've all been well trained not to give in to such clumsy **external** pressures. A much more effective strategy when a friend says "no" to drugs is simply to walk away in mute disgust, and refuse to say a single word to them ever again. By leaving them friendless and alone, you will have created an **internal** pressure that will build, day by day, as their loneliness and despair eat away at them from the inside. Eventually, there is a good chance that they will beg you for a second chance, and far from trying to convince them to try drugs, you will soon be asking them not to **Bogart** your entire stash.

....

FUN CROSSWORD PUZZLE

You can find the answers at the end of this chapter. Remember, no cheating!

Across

1. Movie featuring Keanu Reeves and a bus

3. Dr. Atkins says no to this (abbr.)

6. Cannabis chemical

8. Done to sneakers or corsets

11. ____, ____, ____, Merry Christmas!

12. WWF ____ down

15. "You ____, girl!"

16. ____ browns (great for breakfast)

17. A bigger, uglier mouse

19. He gathers no moss (first name)

22. Where coke addicts meet (abbr.)

23. Jazz vocal improv

26. DisPepsic prostitute

28. Nice friend (first word)

30. Parsley, sage, rosemary, or thyme

33. Ain't ____ ____ shame?

34. Follows NC

36. He holds the cards

37. Angel or devil's food ____

Down

2. It calls the kettle black

3. ____ call (ha ha)

4. Nice friend (second word)

5. He gathers no moss (last name)

7. Corned beef ____ (great for lunch)

9. Which came first, the chicken or the ____

10. Three strikes you're out in ____ ball

13. Let's ____ a Deal

14. Asian Caucasian

18. You're on the right ____

20. "Tits and Ass" (abbr.)

21. The quicker picker-____

24 & 32: ____ ____ or not ____ ____, asks Hamlet.

25. Benevolent feces (first word)

27. Benevolent feces (second word)

28. Prefix meaning 1,000

29. ____otics, e.g., cocaine and heroin

31. Recommended Daily Allowance (abbr.)

35. A roll of the ____

High School

High school is, as its name suggests, an ideal time to start getting high. As soon as you attempt to do this, however, you will learn an important lesson: Doing drugs is easy, but acquiring them can be very difficult.

 DID YOU KNOW? NOT ALL YOUNG BLACK MEN ARE DRUG DEALERS. SOME OF THEM ARE ATHLETES AND DO NOT EVEN DO DRUGS, EXCEPT IN THE OFF-SEASON.

Getting Drugs

The most important thing when buying drugs is to know your vocabulary words, or lingo. When you go to make a buy, **never ask for your drugs by monetary value.** If you say, "Give me $50 worth," the dealer will rip you off and you will deserve it. If, on the other hand, you ask for a "bone" ($50 piece of crack) or a "dove" ($35 piece of crack) or a "boulder" ($20 piece of crack), you will get respect. Practice any words you don't know, so the next time a beat artist tries to burn you with a boulder of bad base, you can beam the bulls over to box him.

NOTE TO WOMEN You are more likely to trade sex for drugs than to buy them, but it is still important to know your street vocabulary. Here is a handy quick-list of useful terms:

Skeezer: Crack ho
Toss-up: Crack ho
Bagbride: Crack ho
Buffer: Woman who trades oral sex for crack
Strawberry: Crack ho
Raspberry: Crack ho

Civic Responsibility

Try to watch a government-sponsored anti-drug advertisement, particularly one that suggests people who buy drugs for personal use are somehow funding terrorist activity. See if you can muster a sense of righteous indignation at these cynical and transparent attempts to shift responsibility for terrorism away from the administration's foreign policy blundering and homeland security ineptitude and onto hapless teenagers like yourself. Can you think what Henry David Thoreau might have said about this? Do you think he would have said that the only way to answer such oppressive outrages is through civil disobedience, that in the face of such blatant hypocrisy it is not only your natural right but also your moral responsibility to do as many "illegal" substances as possible?

Career Counseling

Now that graduation is impending, it is time to start thinking about what you want to do with your life. Fortunately, the "drug track" you began all the way back in junior high can help you make that decision.

Moving on "Up"

If you are on the "uppers" track, you should probably be looking at a career as a Hollywood producer, agent, or director. Uppers provide limitless energy while rendering you incapable of subtlety or taste, and this makes them perfectly suited to an industry in which vast resources are expended to create products of little or no redeeming social value. Also, since you may have been too busy and/or ugly to date attractive people during high school, you will now be able to make up for it by dating young wannabe actors and actresses throughout your Hollywood career.

The Big "Trip"

If you are on the "hallucinogens" track, you will eventually become a starving artist. The artistic medium you choose is not particularly important—you can be a bad painter, a bad poet, a bad musician, or even a bad actor. The essential thing is that you be misunderstood. It is also a good idea to culti-vate the "starving artist" look.

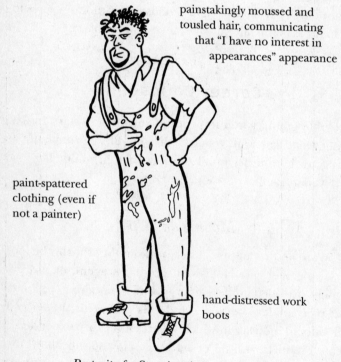

painstakingly moussed and tousled hair, communicating that "I have no interest in appearances" appearance

paint-spattered clothing (even if not a painter)

hand-distressed work boots

Portrait of a Starving Artist

Heroin Chic

If you are on the "downers" track, your career path will ultimately involve prostitution. It is true that this career lacks social prestige, but it does have many benefits for a dedicated heroin user. The payments are in cash, the hours are flexible, and since Johns often fetishize the hyper-skinny look, your emaciated figure will actually help you earn more income.

NOTE Legal but less lucrative forms of prostitution, such as acting and modeling, are also solid career options.

The SAT for Drug Users

Studies have proven that standardized tests are culturally biased against people on drugs. This is a blatant injustice that contributes to the misperception that drug users are stupid and unthinking. Fortunately, we have created a test that balances out the biases. So get out those Number 2 pencils, everyone, and good luck!

MATH
1. *If Dejuan's mother gives him $20 to buy groceries but Dejuan stops off first to buy a dime bag, how much will he have left when he gets to the store?*
   a. $19.90
   b. $10
   c. $10, unless he tries to buy down on Alvarado, in which case that fool's gonna be lucky if they leave him with shoes
2. *It takes Alan 25 minutes to bake a pizza in his oven, and he can bake up to three at a time. It takes Gene just 15 minutes to bake a pizza, but he can only bake one at a time. Once the pizzas are*

baked, it takes Alan 10 minutes to deliver each one, while it takes Gene 12 minutes. If Alan receives an order for seven pizzas, and Gene receives an order for six pizzas but two are to the same location, which one of them will take longer to finish?
    a. Mmmm. . . Pizza
    b. Other

VERBAL

1. *"Baby T" is to "Pee Wee" as:*
    a. "Applejack" is to "Caspar"
    b. "Kangaroo" is to "Johnson"
    c. "Fish Scales" are to "Devil's Dandruff"
    d. All of the above
2. *Which of the sentences below most accurately represents the meaning of the following phrase: "That strawberry bucked a juggler for a biscuit, and Sam put her on ice"?*
    a. That crack whore shot a teenaged drug dealer in the head, and a federal agent put her in jail.
    b. That red seeded fruit unhorsed an ambidextrous entertainer for a British cookie, and a fellow named Sam then took her ice-skating.

LOGIC

1. ☐
    a. This is an empty square. What's the question?
    b. It's like, can you think outside the box, when all they give you is the box? The whole concept of outside the box already depends on the box, so how can you really get outside it, you know? It's like the box is always there whether we realize it or not.
    c. Whoa, that little dinosaur is sliding, man, that's insane.

READING COMPREHENSION

Once upon a time, the author of a timely and relevant social satire attempted to access an informational website in order to gather information for a satiric chapter on drugs. Instead of the desired website, however, what popped up was a DEA logo and a message that said, "This website has been shut down by authority of the United States Drug Enforcement Agency. Your IP address has been logged."

1. *The main point of this selection is that:*
   a. The DEA is kicking some ass! Boo-ya! USA! USA!
   b. The rights of everyday Americans are slowly being eroded by fear-mongering conservative sloganists, and this blatant violation of the right to free speech, chillingly combined with fascist scare tactics that imply that even seeking information can put you on some sort of government suspect list, is yet another step in the current administration's march toward modern McCarthyism.

SOLUTION TO FUN WORD SEARCH (PAGE 59)

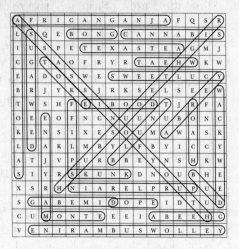

SOLUTION TO FUN CROSSWORD PUZZLE (PAGE 64)

	[1]S	[2]P	E	E	D		[3]C	A	R	[4]B
[5]R	O						R			U
I		[6]T	[7]H	C		[8]L	A	C	[9]E	D
C		A		[10]B		N		G		
[11]H	O		[12]S	[13]M	A	[14]C	K		[15]G	O
A			[16]H	A	S	H				
[17]R	A	[18]T		[19]K	E	I	[20]T	H		[21]U
D		R		E		[22]N	A			P
[23]S	C	A	[24]T			A		[25]G		P
		[26]C	O	K	E	W	H	O	R	E
		K				H		O		R
[27]S				[28]K	I	[29]N	D			
[30]H	E	[31]R	[32]B		[33]I	T	A		[34]O	[35]D
I		[36]D	E	A	L	E	R			I
T		A			O		[37]C	A	K	E

4.

The "Rules" for Dysfunctional Daters

In recent years, much has been written about the "rules" of dating—the ins and outs of attaining a perfect, healthy relationship with a member of the opposite sex. But until now, *nothing* has been written on how to achieve an imperfect, dysfunctional relationship. It's no fun to walk the path of self-destruction alone. Why not take someone down with you? Here, then, are our rules to attaining perfect unhappiness.

Do You Need Our "Rules" for Dating?

Questions for Her

1. *How would you describe the point of dating?*
    a. Getting married
    b. Having fun and meeting new people
    c. Not unlike prostitution, except with payment in the form of oversauced food and theater tickets instead of hard currency

2. *After how many dates would you consider it appropriate for a man to kiss you?*
    a. One
    b. Two
    c. Kissing is rarely if ever appropriate

3. *How would you describe your previous boyfriend?*
    a. Intense
    b. Indifferent
    c. In prison

4. *If you went on an enjoyable date and the guy did not call you within a week, would you:*
    a. Assume he might have lost your number and call him?
    b. Weep daily, wondering why you are so wholly unloveable?
    c. Suspect that demanding a "damage deposit" might have been a mistake?

5. *If the coauthor of a quirky satire such as this one asked you to send him a naked picture of yourself, would you:*
    a. Be offended?
    b. Be flattered?
    c. Send the naked picture to *"Self-Destruction* fan mail, c/o Three Rivers Press, 1745 Broadway, New York, NY 10019"?

Questions for Him

1. *How would you describe the point of dating?*
   a. Getting sex
   b. Other

2. *After how many dates would you expect a woman to sleep with you?*
   a. One
   b. Two
   c. Gay

3. *How would you describe your previous girlfriend?*
   a. An ungrateful slut
   b. A grateful slut
   c. A slut of indeterminate gratitude

4. *If you went on an enjoyable date, how long would you wait to call?*
   a. Call who?

5. *If the coauthor of a quirky satire such as this one wanted to send you a naked picture of herself, would you:*
   a. Be offended?
   b. Be flattered?
   c. Send $5 and a self-addressed stamped envelope to *"Self-Destruction* fan mail, c/o Three Rivers Press, 1745 Broadway, New York, NY 10019"?

SCORING THE QUIZ

Give yourself 5 points for every "A" answer, 10 points for every "B" answer, and 14 points for every "C" answer. Add up your points. The final point total has no predictive or determinative value.

"Her" Introduction

If you are like most single women, you are dating with one simple goal in mind: getting married. Your objective is to find a life partner who will care for you, respect you, and love you for who you really are. In order to accomplish this, you will need to be devious and deceptive, manipulating men in a variety of ways without giving them any true sense of the woman behind the "real you" facade.

Your friends may try to tell you that such an approach is "insane" or "monstrous." They may say that the only way to have a "healthy" relationship is to be honest with your partner, and to treat him with the abiding kindness and enduring respect with which you yourself hope to be treated. But you know better, don't you? You know that women who are honest and kind remain hopelessly single, while those who display flirtatious insouciance and near-sociopathic deceitfulness are awash in suitors and proposals.

The reason for this disparity is that, deep down, men are hunters. They don't want to pursue prey that pursues them back, or prey that simply lies there, dead and maggot-ridden. Rather, they want to experience the thrill of the chase, to bound powerfully after a lithe and unpredictable quarry that seems to elude them at every turn. What they don't know, of course, is that in your case this chase is going to lead them right down the aisle. So, ladies, get ready to **stop pleasing and start teasing.** By following the eight simple Rules we have laid out for you here, you are guaranteed to have a ring on your finger well before most of your friends.

"His" Introduction

If you are like most single men, you are dating with one simple goal in mind: getting sex. Historically, the easiest and most economical way for a man to accomplish this has been to date a "priapic professional," or hooker. While this classic, time-tested approach does involve a hefty up-front fee, it ultimately avoids nearly all of the back-end or "hidden" costs of dating amateurs, such as dinners, drinks, Valentine's Day gifts, abortions, and alimony. And, of course, there is more than mere monetary cost to consider: The emotional price of dating nonprofessionals can often be even higher than the financial cost.

Despite such considerations, however, most twenty-first-century men continue to date amateurs. The same men who would not even consider allowing an amateur mechanic to service their BMWs are stunningly cavalier about allowing rank nonprofessionals to service their genitalia. Clearly, there is something about the fiction of "getting it for free" that men are unable to resist. While we cannot in good conscience recommend this practice, we do recognize that it is inevitably going to continue. With that in mind, we have come up with a set of rules designed to minimize dating risk while maximizing dating gain. So, gentlemen, get ready to **stop paying and start playing.** If you follow the eight simple Rules that we set forth here, you will soon find yourself using dating to attain sex at a considerable fiscal and emotional discount.

The "Rules"

Her Rule #1: Never, Ever Speak to a Man First
....

No matter what your friends tell you, never speak first to a man you are interested in. Remember, men like to pursue seemingly unobtainable women, so the more rude and oblivious you seem, the more men will want you.

Our friend Julie was waitressing in an upscale restaurant when a gentleman came in to dine. Although she only saw him from the back, she immediately noticed that he was dining alone, wearing an expensive suit, and that there was no ring on his finger. She knew right then that he could well be "the one," but she also knew that she could not speak to him first. This was difficult because he was a customer, and her job was to take orders. So what did Julie do? She simply ignored him—first his subtle nod, then his impatient glances, and finally his increasingly frustrated "come hither" gestures. Eventually the man complained to Julie's manager, and she was fired on the spot. As she was leaving the restaurant in tears, an entirely different man stopped her on the street and asked her what was wrong. Well, to make a long story short, they have been dating for almost a year, and we hear that a proposal may be in the works. Enough said?

His Rule #1: Never, Ever Speak to a Woman First

Women will generally attempt to get you to open the conversation. **Do not do it.** Force her to speak first no matter what the cost. Whether you step on her foot or pretend to choke on a chicken bone, you must do something that coerces her into violating the woman's first rule of dating.

One increasingly popular strategy is to pretend initially that you are a deaf-mute, and hand her a card asking for a small donation. Whether or not she gives you money, she will feel compelled to smile and mumble something, anything to appease her own discomfort. Even a brief "here you go" or a simple "I'm sorry, I don't have any change" counts—as soon as she speaks, you can go ahead and drop the deaf-mute pretense and engage her in normal conversation.

Once you have gotten her to break her first rule, it is like removing the cornerstone from a building. Her entire system will crumble like a house of cards, and you will have achieved complete relationship dominance with your opening salvo.

Her Rule #2: Do Not Return His Phone Calls

. . . .

If a man you like calls you, do not pick up the phone and do not return his call. You do not want him to think you are easy to get. One of the most important aspects of the Rules is to make things difficult for him. After all, men love a challenge. If he really likes you he will be willing to lie in wait outside your building, repeatedly stop by your work, scale your fire escape, or find some even more inventive way to interact with you.

Her Rule #3: Do Not Deliver the First Rim Job

. . . .

Rim jobs are a definite no-no for girls who play by the Rules. They are dirty and degrading, and you should not lower yourself to this level unless a man has already done it first.

His Rule #2: Do Not Take Avoidance as a "No"

When a girl seems to be avoiding you and refuses to return your calls, she is simply playing "hard to get"—that is what girls who play by the Rules do. Some might even make things more difficult by changing their address or taking out a **restraining order.** Do not be discouraged; they are simply testing you to see how much you really want to go out with them. The harder you try, the more they like it. Remember that a restraining order is just an order. And really, what woman is attracted to a man who simply follows orders?

His Rule #3: Feel Free to Deliver the First Rim Job

Go ahead, toss that salad. As a man, you are allowed to do degrading things as long as they pave the way to your own sexual gratification.

Her Rule #4: Be the First One to End Every Encounter

You should always be the first one off the phone and the first to say "good night." It is similar to the cardinal rule of comedy: Always leave them wanting a little bit more. This rule is particularly important once the relationship has progressed to the point of physical intimacy. You should always try to "finish" before he does, and then push him off of you immediately. If you allow him to "finish," he will soon be finished with you! If, on the other hand, you keep him constantly on the verge of satisfaction, he will be forever all over you, and give you the attention you crave.

His Rule #4: Pretend You Are Sorry She's Ending the Encounter

Girls who play by the Rules like to end dates early, and boys who play by the Rules are happy to let them. This will allow you to go out with the guys, watch a game, or even make a **booty call** to someone who is actually fun to have sex with. But always make sure that she thinks you are devastated. If you spend even 30 seconds "trying" to talk her into extending the date, she will go away happy and assured of your love for her, instead of jealous and suspicious of what you are doing later that night.

Once your relationship has progressed to the point of physical intimacy, the "pretending" rule is particularly important. The fact is that you will probably "finish" within a very short time, but you should pretend that you did not. Continue to thrust until she finishes and pushes you off. Then pretend that you are distraught, and that you desperately want to continue. Do not let her ascertain that you have already finished, or she may actually want you to stay. As long as you pretend that *you* want to stay, however, she will soon be ushering you out the door, and you can go have a smoke and a beer while watching the late edition of *SportsCenter.*

Her Rule #5: Demand Romantic Valentine's and Birthday Gifts

• •

If he cares about you, he will spend a great deal of his hard-earned cash on a variety of flowers, chocolates, and precious or semi-precious jewels. These presents prove that he loves you and that he is committed to you, and if he gives you anything else, it proves that he does not love you. We know one girl whose supposed boyfriend gave her a portable computer for Valentine's Day. He said it was because she was a writer and he wanted her to be able to work at his place, but we knew that what it really meant was that he did not love her. If he loved her, he would have gotten her a diamond, a romantic red rose, or a box of tasty truffles rather than a brand-new, state-of-the-art, $3,000 Titanium G4. She made him return the computer and buy her diamond earrings, and although they are no longer together, she still has those diamonds.

His Rule #5: Keep Your Receipts

You will occasionally have to buy expensive jewelry in order to keep her from dating other men. As long as you keep the receipts, however, there is no reason you cannot purloin the jewelry back the night before you intend to break up with her. It may sound clichéd to say it, but possession is still nine-tenths of the law, and if you're holding the receipts, what can she say? Chances are she will have too much dignity to take you to small-claims court after the breakup, so you will be free either to return the gifts for cash or to re-box them and give them to someone else.

Her Rule #6: Internet Dating

If you are physically unattractive, then meeting men in bars or clubs is probably not a realistic option. Thank goodness for the Internet! Here you can meet other unfortunate-looking singles and fall in love by comparing lists of the albums, novels, and TV shows each of you thinks will impress the other. You can find out a lot about a person by what books they pretend to love, or what languages they can supposedly speak. Do they also assert that Fellini is their favorite director, or feign a love for Shakespearean comedy? You might be surprised at how much you can pretend to have in common with others. Make sure that you put a lot of thought and hard work into crafting your profile, because men are not just interested in the picture. They also want to spend 30 or 40 seconds getting to know the real you.

Most sites will require that you post a picture with your ad. DO NOT PANIC. As you should know by now, it is always to a girl's advantage to remain diffident and mysterious, and never show too much. We suggest a picture of you in an attractive but tasteful dress, taken from behind. This will give the men some sense of your shape and hair color but will also leave a great deal to the imagination.

His Rule #6: Internet Dating

It is unfortunate that you are unattractive, but unattractiveness is a much greater deficit for women than for men.

In fact, once you are over 30 it can actually be to your advantage to be unattractive. The less attractive you are, the more likely women are to think that you will marry them. As long as they think this, they may well be willing to have sex with you.

HELPFUL HINTS FOR INTERNET DATERS

HER Make sure to include in your profile that you enjoy "walks on the beach," even if you live in a landlocked state such as Oklahoma (walks around Stagner Reservoir are not very romantic).

HIM Always give ironic, glibly inconsequential answers to the profile questions your site asks. You are clearly above this whole Internet dating thing; that's why you're doing it.

HER Try to use the word "soul" as many times as possible in your profile. It can be used as a noun preceded by an adjective ("sensitive soul"), as an adjective modifying a noun ("soulful heart"), and, of course, as part of the more traditional compound noun ("soul mate").

HIM Do not post an attractive picture. Again, you are above this whole Internet dating thing, so it is best to scan in some crappy Polaroid of you drunk and wearing a baseball cap. Women love that.

Movies to Pretend to Like

HER	**HIM**
The Godfather	*Beaches*
Debbie Does Dallas	
Butt Hunt #17	
Barely Legal, Volume III	
Brian's Song	

Her Rule #7: Try to Date
Balding Men over 30

As their hair begins to recede and their middles begin to thicken, men suddenly become much more amenable to the prospect of marriage. The cockiness that they had in their twenties dissipates with each follicle they find on the pillow or in the shower drain; they begin to feel that they may have only a few years left until they are completely bald, and thus wholly unattractive to women. The fact that many women do not mind baldness is immaterial. Men associate hair with masculinity, and you should do everything you can to encourage their anxiety.

This is particularly true if you are already in a relationship but the proposal you long for has not been forthcoming. During intimate moments, try running your fingers through his hair and pausing slightly at the balding spots near the temples. Do not come right out and say that his hair loss bothers you—that will merely make him defensive and withdrawn. Instead, sigh subtly, just enough to remind him that he is in fact losing his hair and had better get you while the getting is good.

Even if he is not losing his hair, it might behoove you to make him think that he is. This can be done by collecting and saving hair from his brush, then putting it on his pillow when he is asleep, or slipping it into the shower while he is shampooing.

His Rule #7: Try to Date
Women over 30

Single women over the age of 30 are desperate, and desperation breeds compromise. They are frantic about getting married, and they know from long experience that wealthy, good-looking men with a full head of hair will not marry them. So, what do they do? They turn to you, of course, never suspecting that you will not marry them, either.

Her Rule #8: Become a Contestant on a Degrading Television Reality Dating Show

One of the best ways to meet a man these days is to get on a show such as *Who Wants to Marry a Millionaire* or *The Bachelor*. True, you will have to compete against twenty or thirty other women in order to wheedle your proposal from a dim-witted narcissist, but those odds are actually much better than what you will face in the everyday world. The fact is that the "bachelors" on these shows are not only photogenic but are also prescreened for STDs and criminal records. A man such as this would in the real world be rabidly pursued by dozens if not hundreds of women, whereas on the reality show you are guaranteed to have at least a 5 percent chance of landing this slightly above-average catch. And, if you follow the other Rules (especially Rule #3—remember the network censors!), your chances will go up even more.

His Rule #8: Try to Date Losing Contestants from Degrading Television Reality Dating Shows

The women who get on these shows are photogenic, have low self-esteem, and will do virtually anything for attention. Many men shy away from dating a "loser," but this is a mistake. Losers tend to be desperate and needy, and even a single judiciously timed compliment could convince an attractive TV loser to go on a date with you.

Of course, she may take on airs now that she has exposed and humiliated herself on national television, but do not attempt to quash this "rock star" sensibility. Rather, you should encourage it. Tell her she looks fantastic on camera, and encourage her to "act" for you while you capture the moment on video. There is an excellent chance that she will be willing to degrade herself in a wide variety of ways as long as you keep the camera rolling.

NOTE Make sure to keep this tape even after you break up with her. Should her anemic career as an actress/model/ spokesperson ever actually take off one day, you will then be able to sell this tape, and your story, for a surprising amount of money.

5.

The Man and Mistress Guide to Infidelity

Test for Men: Is She Cheating on You?

1. *How many partners did she have before she met you?*
   a. 0   (0 POINTS)
   b. 1 or more   (10 POINTS)

2. *Does she wear makeup even when you are not present?*
   a. No   (0 POINTS)
   b. Yes   (10 POINTS)

3. *Has she ever commented favorably on the looks of an actor or television personality?*
   a. No   (0 POINTS)
   b. Yes   (10 POINTS)

4. *When she returns home from work, how does she smell?*
   a. Fresh, virginal   (0 POINTS)
   b. Smoky, used   (10 POINTS)

5. *(Muslim-specific) When she goes to fetch water, does she:*
   a. Cover body and face in traditional fashion?   (0 POINTS)
   b. Cover body and face in modern fashion?   (5 POINTS)
   c. Shame self and family by inadvertently   (25 POINTS)
   exposing swatch of skin to covetous gaze of infidel?

SCORING THE QUIZ

If zero points, she may well be cheating on you, but she's sneaky. If 5 or more points, not only is she cheating, she also doesn't care if you know it.

••

Test for Women: Is He Cheating on You?
Yes.

Hail the Infidels

Man or woman, young or old, straight or gay, there is nothing more exciting than illicit sex with a partner you simultaneously lust for and loathe. Adulterous sex can be one of the most fulfilling forms of self-degradation, and the best part is you don't need a lot of skill or experience in order to get started. In fact, anyone willing to put time and effort into learning the simple skills we set forth here can become an accomplished infidel.

Man and Mistress

There are many forms of infidelity, but the most archetypal, enduring, and mutually self-destructive is that between man and mistress. From Antony and Cleopatra to Bill and Monica, the relationships between men and their mistresses have destroyed more lives and careers than all other forms of adultery combined. The goal of this chapter is to help both men and women to begin and maintain a mutually destructive man/mistress relationship.

Some parts of this chapter are geared to the respective needs of either man or mistress, but this does not mean that women should not read the "Man" sections, and vice versa. In fact, it is often very enlightening to get a perspective on the way that the other half approaches infidelity.

 DID YOU KNOW? THIRTY-TWO OF THE 43 U.S. PRESIDENTS HAD AT LEAST ONE MISTRESS. THOSE WHO DID NOT–VAN BUREN, CARTER, AND GEORGE W. BUSH, FOR EXAMPLE–ARE GENERALLY PERCEIVED AS "UNCOOL."

Getting Started—Men

For men, getting started is usually the most difficult part. It is okay if you feel nervous or inadequate. After all, convincing a woman to sleep with you is difficult enough to begin with. Doing it when you're already in a fully committed relationship with someone else can seem next to impossible.

For this reason, it is generally best to approach someone you have power over. A student, for example, if you are a teacher. A junior employee might be the right target for a business executive, while a prisoner or parole violator could be appropriate if you've built a career in law enforcement.

 DID YOU KNOW? IN MOST SEXUAL AFFAIRS BETWEEN BOSSES AND EMPLOYEES, THE EMPLOYEES SAY THEY FELT "POWERLESS" TO REFUSE.

Using Your Child as Bait

Perhaps the biggest infidelity fallacy is that children are a hindrance to finding a mistress. There is nothing that women—even slutty adulterous ones—find more attractive than a father with a child, especially a girl. Through a process called **transference** the woman will unconsciously imagine you as the father she always wanted—and, ironically, it won't be long before you're teaching her some memorable lessons about what happens when she talks to strangers.

The Sweetest Taboo

It does not matter how much you lie, cajole, and manipulate in order to get your chosen mistress to sleep with you for the first time. Once she has broken the adultery taboo, she may well find that she likes it, and your initial lies will be forgiven.

Getting Started—Women

Please, you're a woman. Approach any heterosexual male and indicate you're available. He will take you up on the offer.

Once you've found a partner, it is important to cultivate the **mistress look.** This will not only enable you to feel as if you are someone other than yourself (the key to rationalization), but it will conveniently provide you with all the equipment you'll need to conduct your illicit affair worry-free.

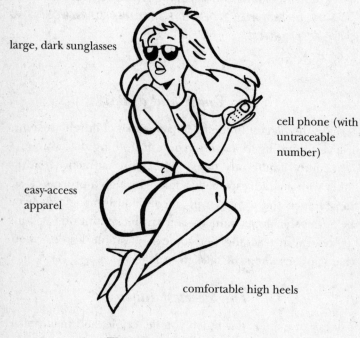

large, dark sunglasses

cell phone (with untraceable number)

easy-access apparel

comfortable high heels

The Mistress Look

INFIDELITY SURVEY

FAVORITE PLACES TO HAVE ADULTEROUS SEX

Restroom at work: 8%

Vegas: 14%

Car: 20%

Cheap hotel down
   road: 27%

In the butt: 31%

LEAST FAVORITE PLACES

Porta Potti: 1%

Nebraska: 4%

On camera: 22%

Expensive hotel down
   road: 25%

In the sanctity of marriage
   bed: 48%

Man and Mistress Together
Avoiding Clear Communication

Clear communication is the death knell of any dysfunctional relationship and should be avoided if at all possible. A mistress should never ask direct questions, such as "Are you going to leave your wife?" because if the answer is "no," she will then be stuck with very little room for self-delusion. Instead, she might try asking, "Couldn't you see us on a beach in Maui?" To this he will likely say "yes," because he's thinking about seven straight days of sex written off as a business expense, and she will then be free to fantasize that both he and she are envisioning a romantic honeymoon.

On the following pages are some telling examples of what infidels say, what their partners hear, and what they really mean:

He Said, She Said

He says	*She hears*	*He means*
I'm not going to leave my wife.	I'd leave my wife if only you were a little bit thinner.	*I'm not going to leave my wife, but the thinner you are, the better.*
The fact is, you and I are too different to ever work as a couple.	Savannah fastened the diamond necklace just as Hans burst into the boudoir. The rakishly handsome groundskeeper was smudged with sweat and grime, his eyes dark with purpose. Though Savannah had often watched him riding from her window, his flesh rippling in rhythm with the beasts as his thighs guided their movements, she had never spoken to him. Yet, somehow, he knew. Her cheeks flamed at the thought. "How dare you!" she cried, her ivory breasts heaving indignantly. But he paid her no heed. He moved upon her like a beast, his strong hands seizing her tiny corseted waist and his full mouth muffling her protests. As though in a dream her rebel lips opened, inviting him to claim her.	*If I left her and married you, I'd cheat on you.*

She Said, He Said

She says	He hears	She means
I want to talk about our relationship.	I want you to take my clothes off and do unconscionable things to me.	*I want to talk about our relationship.*
This relationship isn't right. We have to stop.	I want some really expensive jewelry.	*I want some really expensive jewelry.*
So . . . did you see what happened on the NASDAQ today?	I want you to take my clothes off and do unconscionable things to me.	*I'm lonely, tired, and PMS-ing, and if you bring that pathetic semi-erection anywhere near me, I will chop it off and feed it to my cat.*

Man and Mistress "Troubleshooting" Guide

Here are some simple solutions to common problems you may encounter.

Mistress

PROBLEM You call, his wife answers, and you hang up in a panic.

SOLUTION Your phone will immediately begin ringing because she's suspicious and has hit *69. DO NOT pick it up. Immediately unplug your answering machine so that the phone continues to ring. Let it keep ringing. From now on you will not be able to answer your phone or use your answering machine.

Man

PROBLEM Mistress repeatedly calls and hangs up on suspicious wife.

SOLUTION Go on the offensive. Ask wife who that was on the phone. When she says she doesn't know, pretend you don't believe her. When she tries to hit *69, grab the phone away jealously and say, "I'll get to the bottom of this."

Man

PROBLEM Mistress says she is pregnant.

SOLUTION No solution needed. She's lying. Mistresses are engineered for your pleasure and thus never have periods, pregnancies, or excessive pubic hair.

Mistress

PROBLEM You told him you're pregnant, and he called your bluff.
SOLUTION Two words: BJ.

Man

PROBLEM You give your wife an STD you picked up from your mistress.
SOLUTION Again, go on the offensive. Accuse your wife of picking up the disease and deny having it yourself. If she threatens to leave you, simply respond, "Go ahead. No one's going to want you, you diseased whore."

Mistress

PROBLEM He's never going to leave his wife.
SOLUTION Pick up an STD, and hope when he passes it on to his wife she'll leave him.

GIRL POWER

Women, if you discover that your man is cheating on you, do not even consider leaving him until you've had at least one revenge affair. The fact is, you might find the revenge more enjoyable than the actual relationship.

Revenge Affairs That Really Hurt

AN EX An ex-boyfriend is the most obvious mark, but there is a chance that your plan will backfire. Many women talk down the sexual abilities of their previous boyfriend so as not to intimidate their current partner. Should you then take up with the man previously labeled a sexual incompetent, your partner may feel amusement and pity instead of abject rage and existential impotence.

A FOREIGNER No matter how low an American man may feel, he can always reassure himself with the knowledge that he is superior to the men of other nations. By getting involved with a foreigner, you take that away from him. Different foreigners can do different kinds of damage, but if you really want to hurt your man, go with a Frenchman.

A Typical "Foreigner"

YOUR BOSS Your boss is a man who wields power over you and whom you inherently want to please, so your

partner is already anxious about him. He probably cou
ters these beta-male anxieties with a secret suspicion
that, while he's not as successful professionally as your
boss, he is younger and better-looking and more profi-
cient sexually. The knowledge that your boss uses and
abuses you for his sexual gratification could well be
enough to emasculate your man completely.

ANYONE WITH A MOTORCYCLE Frankly, we don't know
why this works, but it works. Trust us. The thought of you
riding some other guy's hog will make him insane.

HIS BEST FRIEND It's dirty, it's cruel, and it's the Holy
Grail of revenge affairs. Best friends always compete over
women, but the real winner of this competition is you.

....

DID YOU KNOW? SEVEN PERCENT OF AMERICAN CHILDREN ARE
NOT THE OFFSPRING OF THEIR SUPPOSED FATHERS.

In the End

Getting Caught

Always assume when having an affair that you will eventually get caught, and prepare your rebuttal strategy beforehand. For men, the strategy is simple: Deny everything. No matter what she says or what evidence she has, swear on all that is holy that you did not do it. Remember, your wife's capacity for self-delusion is at least equal to that of your mistress.

For women, the strategy is slightly different. You are probably having the affair to hurt your man on some level, so don't give him the satisfaction of a flat-out denial. Instead, slyly **refuse to give any direct answers,** and, whenever possible, **turn his questions around on him.** This way he will be tortured with doubts, yet cling surreally to the idea that you remain innocent and chaste. Remember, the only thing more self-deluding than a desperate woman is a desperate man.

His/Hers Interrogation Answers

Are you cheating on me?

HIM: No.   HER: Are you serious?

I know you're cheating on me.

HIM: You're wrong. I'm not.   HER: How?

I have pictures of you in bed with Joyce.

HIM: Can't be me; I don't   HER: Why would I sleep with a
    know any Joyce.   man named Joyce?

Joyce is my best friend!

HIM: Oh, Joyce. Nope, didn't sleep with her.

HER: Are you sure he's your best friend?

How could you betray me like this?

HIM: I didn't betray you.

HER: *You're* betraying *me* by not trusting me.

Do you swear to God you're not cheating on me?

HIM: Absolutely. May the Lord strike me down if I'm lying.

HER: It wouldn't mean anything. I don't believe in God.

Do you love me?

HIM: Yes, more than anything.

HER: What do you think, silly?

6.

Condoms Are for Suckers

Are You Ready for Sex?

1. *How old are you?*
   a. 8–10
   b. 10–12
   c. Old enough

2. *Have you ever experienced feelings of attraction for an older man?*
   a. Gross
   b. Maybe . . . sometimes . . . I don't know . . .
   c. You mean, like, Father Miller?

3. *What time do your parents get home from work?*
   a. 5:00
   b. 6:00
   c. My dad left for work two years ago, and he still hasn't come home.

4. *What are you wearing?*
   a. My school uniform
   b. Roller skates
   c. What are *you* wearing?

5. *If $200 and a plane ticket arrived at your house in an unmarked envelope, would you:*
   a. Report it to the authorities?
   b. Throw away the ticket and spend the money at the mall?
   c. Not even consider getting on that plane for less than $500?

SCORING THE QUIZ

If you answered "A" or "B" to most of the above questions, you are not quite ready yet—but don't worry, this chapter will get you prepared in no time! If you answered "C" to three or more questions, it is vitally important that you call 1-900-879-6734 and ask for Chico.

A Time of Discovery

Sexual intercourse is one of the most beautiful things two people can share. Though many people feel societal pressure either to engage in or refrain from sexual activity, the truth is there is no compelling reason either to rush into it or to avoid it. Being a virgin is nothing for you to be ashamed of, and neither is passing out and getting "long-boned" by members of your school's football or basketball team. Both are simply natural, physical ways of expressing your own unique personality.

If you do decide that sexual activity is something you would like to pursue, then it is important to prepare yourself by understanding your options. In this chapter we will offer you information on everything from foreplay to "end" play, and we will also attempt to deflate some of the myths surrounding human sexuality with our Myth Buster sections.

Topiary of the World

Before engaging in sex, it is important to make sure you are well groomed. While American women have traditionally just shaved or waxed around the line of their bikini bottoms, there are many exciting international forms of topiary from which to choose, and we have illustrated six of the most popular ones on the facing page.

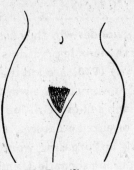

The Brazilian

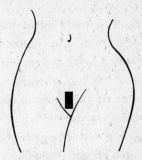

The German (also known as the inverted Hitler)

The African

The Orthodox

The Canadian

The Persian

MYTH BUSTER: THE FEMALE "ORGASM"

....

Incredibly, many women actually wonder why they are "inorgasmic," not realizing that the female orgasm is actually a myth created in the early 1970s, around the time of the "equal opportunity" movement, as a way for women to gain control over a man's self-esteem. The premise is simple: Men are goal-oriented creatures, and by giving men the goal of creating an "orgasm," women set up a classic Pavlovian manipulation scenario. If and only if the man behaves in exactly the way a woman wishes, moving his exhausted tongue and trembling fingers for long periods of time according to her exact specifications, she will reward him with an "orgasm" routine that consists of fast breathing, a few *Oh Gods*, and then a slight tensing of the thigh muscles accompanied by some sort of moan or sigh. Over the years, American men have grown so fixated on achieving this dubious reward that it has become integral to their sense of masculinity. While there is no physical evidence that these "orgasms" actually exist, they have nonetheless proven a remarkably effective tool in manipulating the egos of insecure men.

....

Foreplay

One of the most important aspects of human sexuality is called **foreplay.** Foreplay generally precedes sexual intercourse, and it can be verbal, visual, or physical in nature.

Verbal Foreplay, or "Pillow Talk"

Talking "dirty" can be an extremely effective method of foreplay. But it is important to remember that men and women like different things. Men like to keep it simple. Women, on the other hand, love stories. They also like to feel comfortable, so a man engaging in verbal foreplay would do well to think of a place where his partner feels safe and at ease, and set the story there.

SAMPLE PILLOW TALK FOR HIM "We're in Grandma's house. It's got that great grandma smell, and grandma's baking cookies. There are family pictures on the wall: Joey and Petey and the twins and Aunt Maggie. Snuggles the cat is sleeping on the piano, and under the piano there's a dirty little slut with her mouth wrapped around a big . . ."

SAMPLE PILLOW TALK FOR HER "Harder."

 DID YOU KNOW? THE AVERAGE MAN THINKS ABOUT SEX ONCE EVERY SEVEN SECONDS, AND ABOUT THE LONG-HAIRED AFRICAN ORANGUTAN ONCE EVERY 14.2 YEARS.

MYTH BUSTER: THE G-SPOT
....

Contrary to popular belief, there is no such thing as a
G-spot. The term actually derives from the street-slang
name for a $1,000 bill. It is well documented that any
time a man spends a thousand or more dollars on a
woman—whether on jewelry, theater tickets, or even just
a simple cash gift—the next time they have sex she will
thrash, moan, and achieve an impressive "orgasm" (see
previous Myth Buster). Somewhere along the line, men
who could not afford to spend a thousand dollars created
the "end of the rainbow" myth that the G-spot is actually
a physical place inside of a woman, and that those who
find it will "please" their women as much as men who are
willing to spend a thousand dollars on them. This is pure
fiction.

....

The Look of Love

Humans are extremely visual creatures, and simply gazing into the eyes of an attractive partner can be one of the best ways to get yourself "in the mood." Unfortunately, most people will, through a lack of options, be forced to have intercourse with a partner who is less than attractive. This may be due to facial misalignment, acne, or even an unsightly and distracting mole. Whatever the reason, the important thing is to use one of the following techniques to distract yourself from the offending visual stimulus.

TECHNIQUE FOR HIM Bagging. Place a grocery bag over your partner's head prior to coitus. This simple but effective technique allows for full visual attention to the body without any distractions from a partner's unfortunate visage.

TECHNIQUE FOR HER Visualization. Visualize your partner with a bag over his head.

You've Got the Touch

Physical foreplay can take the form of either manual or oral stimulation. Although there are many sources of advice on how to deliver physical foreplay, there is a dearth of advice on how best to receive these "gifts." Receiving will therefore be the focus of our advice section.

RECEIVING MANUAL STIMULATION: HIM Frankly, there are few things less appetizing than a girl with a bag on her head clumsily manipulating your member. It is important, however, that you pretend to enjoy the HJ, because her sense of success will encourage her to explore more ways of pleasuring you.

RECEIVING MANUAL STIMULATION: HER As anyone with even a remedial knowledge of female anatomy should know, pleasure comes from being touched on the external genitalia, not from having a finger inserted into the vagina. Yet the practice continues. Why? Though men claim to engage in this maneuver to please you, what they are in fact doing is engaging in a scouting expedition, checking the area for any obstacles that might impede entry (i.e., a hymen, tampon, or carefully tucked penis). You will probably notice that after this initial foray, they will never feel a need to touch the area again.

RECEIVING ORAL STIMULATION: HER (Cunnilingus, aka Compensation) Oral stimulation by an enthusiastic and knowledgeable partner can be one of the most direct routes to "orgasm." Unfortunately, however, there is an inverse relationship between a man's affinity for cunnilingus and the size of his penis. Accordingly, many women find that rather than being able to relax and enjoy the efforts of an orally talented partner, they instead find themselves **distracted by dread** over the inevitable emergence of his inadequate member. The best thing to do in this situation is to focus on the **feeling,** not on the **future.**

RECEIVING ORAL STIMULATION: HIM (The BJ) As evidenced in many pornographic films, there are few things that arouse a woman more than having something **large and hard** shoved repeatedly into her larynx. Your partner may be shy about seeking this pleasure for fear of appearing too greedy or sexually aggressive. If she seems tentative, you can let her know it's okay to indulge by placing both palms behind her head and firmly pressing it down onto your erect member. Watch for such signs of pleasure as gurgles and "gagging" noises.

ETIQUETTE CORNER

....

Dear Ms. Manners:

I recently attended a wedding, along with most of my family and a few old acquaintances. It was a church ceremony, and since we had arrived early and had some extra time, I ducked into one of the confessional booths with this boy I knew from high school so we could "amuse" ourselves. Well, to make a long story short, he walked out with a big smile on his face, and I walked out with sticky wet residue all over my hair. The question is, was it okay for me in this instance to wear my hat during the ceremony? My mother and my aunt say "no," that it was inexcusable for me to wear a hat in the church no matter what, while my father says that covering up the evidence of my sin was by far the most important thing. Please help us, Ms. Manners; we're living in a house divided.

> *Sincerely,*
> **Should Have Swallowed in Seattle**

....

Dear "Should Have,"

You're a whore. That said, the appropriate thing in this instance would have been to wait outside with your hat on until after the wedding party entered, then take your hat off and sit at the very back of the church where no one could behold your disgrace.

....

"In the End"

Unwanted pregnancy is no joke, and we encourage you not to risk it. Sometimes, however, abstinence is just not an option, and in such cases we suggest that you try "ass-tinence." Anal sex drastically lowers risk of pregnancy, and it can still be a beautiful experience if and when you get over the searing pain of initial entry.

THE MEADOWLARK Move toward the vagina as though attempting normal rear entry, but then, at the last possible moment, enter the rectum with a decisive thrust.

THE DONKEY PUNCH The Donkey Punch is a relatively simple maneuver. When engaged in anal sex from behind, simply punch your partner in the back of the neck so that the sphincter clenches up. Note: The element of surprise adds a great deal of intensity to the clench, so try to disguise from your partner the fact that a Donkey Punch is imminent.

THE HOUDINI The Houdini offers a magical twist on the finish from behind. Pull out of your partner a few seconds before you normally would, moan intensely, and spit on her back. When she then turns around for a post-coital embrace, let go in her face, and she will wonder how you did it.

ONE FOR THE GIRLS: THE BELGIAN SPRITZER If your man is a master of the Meadowlark, consider surprising him in return with this "European" delight. When you go into the bathroom for your pre-anal-sex enema, insert the enema as you normally would but do not release it. This time, when he Meadowlarks his way in, he'll be in for a sexy surprise of his own.

Your STD and You

For too long, STD sufferers felt they could not tell others about their condition. They feared judgment, finger pointing, even laughter. But things have changed, and there is no longer any reason to feel ashamed, or to keep your disease a secret. Be proud of who you are, and of what you have. When first meeting people, try letting them know about your disease—talk about your symptoms, and how you acquired it. You may find that nothing breaks the ice like a classic STD anecdote!

STDs can also open up a whole new world of dating. From chat rooms devoted to herpes sufferers to the ointment section of your local pharmacy, there are lots of places to connect with STD singles just like yourself.

And one other thing: If you find yourself attracted to someone who is (or claims to be) STD-free, don't despair. Let them know about your condition, and present them with the following list.

Reasons to Date Someone with an STD
  1. Low self-esteem
  2. Slutty
  3. Might cheat on you, but that guy is fucked
  4. Sterility—no chance of pregnancy
  5. It is actually kind of fun to say "chlamydia"
  6. Good chance of getting them on the angry rebound
  7. More sensitive—at least in the genital area
  8. Probably figures, "What's one more bad decision?"

7.

How to Lose Way Too Much Weight in 90 Days

Do You Need to Lose Weight?

1. *How many calories do you consume per day?*
   a. 200–300
   b. 400–500
   c. 600 or more

2. *Do you consider Calista Flockhart to be:*
   a. Grossly overweight?
   b. Slightly overweight?
   c. About right?

3. *How many days a week do you work out?*
   a. 7
   b. 6
   c. Less than 6

4. *If you could be one of the following vegetables, which would you be?*
   a. A string bean
   b. A wizened carrot
   c. Kale

5. *Would you describe your butt as:*
   a. An "innie"?
   b. Skeletal?
   c. An "outie"?

SCORING THE QUIZ

If you answered "A" to all five questions, congratulations! You already have a serious eating disorder, and this chapter will be mostly review for you. If you answered "B" or "C" to any questions, you probably retain some vestigial sense of proportion, and should read this chapter with careful attention. If you answered "C" to three or more questions, you are a corpulent cow undeserving of love.

The "Skinny"

We're going to be straight with you, right from the start. This chapter provides you with all the information you'll need to lose a jaw-dropping amount of weight, but it isn't going to be easy. There will be emotional distress, physical discomfort, and possibly even medical and psychological interventions for you to contend with.

 FAT FACT: NEARLY HALF OF ALL DRASTIC WEIGHT REDUCTION PROGRAMS ARE FORESTALLED BY "CONCERNED" FRIENDS AND RELATIVES BEFORE ULTIMATE WEIGHT-LOSS GOALS ARE MET.

Some people you now think of as friends may grow uncomfortable as the pounds come off. Those who consider themselves slim and attractive may even unconsciously try to hinder you as you become the more attractive one. They may ask, order, or beg you to eat something—requests that will be difficult to refuse when you have been weakened by hunger. Probably the most important thing in a program of drastic weight reduction is either to isolate yourself completely or to make sure you are surrounded by a set of people who will support you no matter what.

DID YOU KNOW? *JOINING A SORORITY INCREASES YOUR CHANCE OF DEVELOPING AND MAINTAINING AN EATING DISORDER BY 130 PERCENT.*

Staying the Course

The essential thing is that you not give up! If you stick with our three-month program through thick and thin (and thinner!), you will develop eating and exercising habits that have the power to:

1. Consume so much of your time and attention that all your other problems will simply seem unimportant
2. Garner attention from people who would otherwise ignore you
3. Appease that insistent inner voice that says you don't deserve anything good in your life, even food

If you give us three months—three months, three simple stages—we will change your life.

Are you ready? Grab a Diet Coke and let's get to it.

Month 1: Stop Eating

For the first month, your goal will be to stop eating. Sounds easy, doesn't it? You will probably find that it is not as simple as it sounds.

FAT FACT: EIGHTY-SEVEN PERCENT OF ALL DIETERS SAY THAT EATING IS THE BIGGEST HINDRANCE TO ACHIEVING THEIR WEIGHT-LOSS GOALS.

One reason it is difficult to stop eating is that we are constantly barraged by cues telling our brain it is time to eat. Stimuli that may make you reach for that knife and fork could include the smell of food cooking, the sound of a dinner bell, or soul-wrenching hunger.

Each of these is an example of what we call a **conditioning stimulus.** It is difficult for any of us not to respond to a lifetime of conditioning, so a good idea is to develop substitute responses to the conditioning stimuli. For example, when you wake up in the morning, reach for a cigarette instead of a bagel.

FAT FACT: SMOKERS WEIGH ON AVERAGE SEVEN POUNDS LESS THAN NONSMOKERS.

The next time you are confronted with a stimulus that tells you to eat, take it as a challenge. Try to distract yourself as long as you can. Can you go an hour before giving in? Eight hours? A whole day?

Meal Planner, Month 1

DAY 1
Breakfast: Just kidding

Lunch: Diet Coke
Preparation: Remove Diet Coke from refrigerator. Tap light on top of can (this does nothing to release carbonation but does burn a calorie or two). Open can. Pour in glass over ice and drink at your leisure. If still hungry, eat ice.

Afternoon Snack: Diet Coke
Preparation: Same as lunch.

Dinner: Skittles
Preparation: Tear open packet and pour Skittles into bowl. Eat one at a time, alternating by color as desired. As you consume each Skittle, make sure to remind yourself that it is ten calories of pure cellulite. Test yourself each night to see how many Skittles you can leave in the bowl.

Nighttime Snack: Caffeine-Free Diet Coke
Preparation: Same as lunch, but no ice.

DAYS 2–30
Repeat Day 1.

Brainwashing

It's strange to hear people talk about brainwashing as if it's a bad thing. After all, you wouldn't let your armpits go for weeks without washing, would you? Or your hair? Or even your car? Of course you wouldn't. In fact, there is a good chance that you clean yourself and your surroundings daily, obsessively even, and are in fact washing your hands right now. Yet, somehow, society has convinced us that it's okay to let our brains go for months or even years without a good scrub. Clearly, this needs to change.

We have developed a very simple brainwashing method called the **"Change . . . To" technique.** The idea is that you take old, dirty, imperfect ideas and emotions and change them into new, clean, perfect ideas and emotions. It's like changing your clothes after a week of camping—you will feel so much better. Are you ready to give it a try?

Change . . .	*To . . .*
I feel like a failure.	My failure can be used as revenge against my parents.
I feel like I'm spinning out of control.	Spinning burns 300 calories an hour!
I feel desperately alone.	Hunger is my friend.
I feel inadequate when I look at the myriad personal and career successes of others.	Whatever. At least I'm not fat.

Getting the idea? Feel free to invent some more on your own. The important thing is that from now on, you are going to practice a program of good psychic hygiene, and cleanse your mind with the "Change . . . To" technique for at least 60 minutes each day.

INSTEAD OF EATING . . .

1. Look in the mirror. Try to notice small defects such as freckles and blackheads.
2. Try on clothes from childhood.
3. Remove any unnecessary body hair with tweezers.
4. Make balloon animals.
5. Find an obese person; observe them narrowly.

....

* *Inspiration Corner* *

Flesh melts, snow in spring,

father's furrowed brow

triumph

....

Month 2: Exercising Your Demons

You did it, didn't you? Sometime during your first month you went on an eating binge. Did you feel guilty and worthless afterward? Don't worry. Guilt and self-loathing are normal, inevitable, and, believe it or not, useful! These feelings are your inner demons, and they will be essential to driving your exercise activities in Month Two of the program. Don't ignore your inner demons; listen to them. What are they saying? They know a lot about you, don't they? Now, listen to us. You don't need an exorcist to appease these demons—you just need an exercycle!

More Equals Better

It's basic math: If a little exercise is good, then more is obviously better. In fact, your mantra this month will be that you cannot possibly exercise too much. You need to start letting those inner demons push you. If you normally do an hour on the StairMaster after a meal, try upping that to an hour and a half. It's all a question of discipline.

 DID YOU KNOW? HIGH-SCHOOL WRESTLERS ARE ABLE TO LOSE UP TO 12 POUNDS IN A SINGLE DAY SIMPLY BY SPITTING INCESSANTLY INTO A CUP.

The "Fat You" Workout Partner

During your workouts, it is important to stay focused and intense. Some people use a workout partner or personal trainer for this, but those people are weak. You do not need to hire a personal trainer, because your workout partner is the inner demon of shame and humiliation locked deep inside you. Your partner is the "fat you." You hate the "fat you," and the "fat you" hates you.

Visualization is the key to utilizing the "fat you." During a kickboxing workout, for instance, imagine that you are punching the "fat you" in the face. Look at your fat face grinning at you. Hit that fat face. While aerobicizing, imagine that you are kicking and stepping on the "fat you" while it is down.

YOU

FAT YOU

The All-Day Workout

Most of you are already old hands at traditional workout methods. But we'd like to ask you something you may not have thought of before: Why should free weights, aerobics classes, and a couple of hours on the StairMaster be the extent of your day's exercise? Here are some tips on how to make exercise an all-day adventure:

KEEP MOVING One of the best "tricks of the trade" is to be always moving, even when you're sitting. In a business meeting, for example, tap your feet incessantly, and make as many gratuitous gesticulations as possible. You don't see Tony Robbins with any extra pounds on him, do you? This technique also works well at restaurants and on airplanes.

ADD WEIGHT TO TAKE OFF WEIGHT Wear wrist and ankle weights everywhere. If this feels inappropriate, consider matching them to shoe and shirt color.

WORKOUT PARTIES Try to organize your social engagements around workout activities. Things that used to involve cake, alcohol, and other calorie-laden foodstuffs can easily be turned into opportunities for weight loss. Consider, for example, a bar mitzvah 10K or an anniversary swim. Instead of cake and ice cream, a fifth birthday jog could be a wonderful treat for both you and your child—after all, it's never too early for children to develop good weight-loss habits.

DRESS FOR SUCCESS Wear Spandex workout clothes that are a size or two too small—this will keep your demons howling and push you to push yourself. Also, try to wear your workout clothes at all times, not just when you are actually working out. A date, for example, or a friend's baby shower, or even "casual Fridays" could be good opportunities to appear in your too-tight Spandex.

Infomercials

There is a vital mental and emotional support system out there that most of us overlook: **celebrity spokespeople.** During Month Two, we want you to watch a few exercise infomercials, and try to believe the claims they make. As you are watching, remember that these spokespeople are second- and third-tier celebrities, and as such they definitely care about your well-being. They would never try to sell you something unless it had actually worked for them and their friends.

As you debate pulling out your credit card, remember this: Any dollar you spend on exercise gadgets is a dollar you won't be able to spend on food.

 FAT FACT: TAKEN IN LARGE DOSES, DIET DRUGS SUCH AS PHEN-PHEN HAVE BEEN SHOWN TO CAUSE KIDNEY DISEASE. KIDNEY DISEASE IS RELATIVELY PAINLESS, AND PEOPLE WITH KIDNEY DISEASE WEIGH ON AVERAGE 12 POUNDS LESS THAN THOSE WITHOUT KIDNEY DISEASE.

Measuring Yourself

Now that you're well into the program, it is important to find realistic yardsticks by which to measure your progress. Here are two handy measuring sticks.

1. Read any fashion magazine, and compare your body to the bodies of the models. Do you look similar? If not, use that as motivation. These models have cultivated perfect figures, so it's not unrealistic to assume that you can, too.

2. Go to the beach, and observe pre-teen girls and boys as they frolic in the waves. You'll note that many of these pre-teens seem almost effortlessly lithe. This is what you are ultimately attempting to uncover: your inner child-body.

PURGATION: THE GREAT DEBATE
· ·

Since the time of the Roman Empire, purgation has
been a useful substitute when exercise is not possible.
The debate rages on, however, over the relative
merits of oral vs. anal purgation.

Vomiting Side Effects: Negative	Vomiting Side Effects: Positive
Bad breath	Get really skinny
Tooth decay	
Esophageal hemorrhage	
Organ damage	
Death	

Laxative Side Effects: Negative	Laxative Side Effects: Positive
Abdominal cramping	Get really skinny
Flatulence	
Explosive diarrhea	
Organ damage	
Death	

Month 3: Advanced Techniques

By now you've begun to lose some serious weight. But you've probably also realized how many obstacles there are to reaching your weight-loss goals. It's one thing to avoid eating when at home by yourself, but how do you avoid it when out on a date? Or at a holiday party? Or during a psychological intervention? Not to worry. In this final section, we anticipate the problems you will face and provide you with some innovative solutions.

Innovative Problem Solving

PROBLEM You are on a date, and an expensive dinner arrives.

SOLUTION Food purse
Forget makeup, Chapstick, breath mints, and other attractiveness aids. Remember that no one will want you if you're fat anyway, so staying stick thin must be your first priority. With that in mind, empty your purse completely before your date and line it with a plastic bag. This is your *food purse*. Whenever your date is not looking, simply slip food into the food purse, and dispose of it later.

For men, the *food wallet* is an option, but generally only works with prosciutto, sashimi, or other thinly sliced solids. Soup is obviously a no-no, so avoid ordering it.

PROBLEM There's a week left before the beauty pageant, and you've still got a thin layer of subcutaneous fat.

SOLUTION Stomach virus or intestinal parasite
It is surprisingly easy to pick up both viruses and parasites at any hospital. Simply find a gastroenterologist and surrepti-

tiously follow him on his rounds. Take small nibbles from the discarded food trays of his patients.

PROBLEM Family food gathering (especially during holiday season)

SOLUTION Food poisoning
Families make it virtually impossible to avoid eating. Everyone brings a dish, there's food everywhere, and eating is sometimes the only alternative to talking to relatives. Make sure that your dish involves mayonnaise, and let it sit in the sun for several hours before the gathering. Under any other circumstance mayonnaise is a weight-loss no-no, but in this case it is justified, as it provides a fertile breeding ground for bacteria. This technique not only helps you lose weight, but also provides hours of entertainment as your relatives unwittingly participate in your weight-loss program. (Note: Unless you enjoy cleanup, make sure the party is not at your house.)

PROBLEM The intervention

SOLUTION Run
You've been summoned to what you think will be just another family get-together, and it turns out to be a surprise intervention. Don't worry. This happens to everyone. As your friends and relatives make their declarations to you, nod thoughtfully, as though you are pensive and ashamed, and **do not look anyone in the eye.** As soon as an opportunity presents itself, run.

 DID YOU KNOW? A PERSON WITH A GRAM OF COCAINE IN THEIR SYSTEM BURNS UP TO 60 PERCENT MORE CALORIES THAN SOMEONE WHO IS SUPPOSEDLY "CLEAN."

Success

Congratulations! Once you've made it through your intervention, you've clearly acquired enough self-destructive habits and weight-loss acumen to keep the cycle going on your own.

Remember, the world is a complex place, but your weight-loss goals are reassuringly simple. If anything in your life ever starts to feel out of control, just slow down and remember the three simple steps you've learned in these pages: Stop eating, exercise your demons, and practice innovative weight-loss problem solving.

Good luck!

ONE FOR THE BOYS
....

Advantages of dating a woman with an eating disorder:
1. She's a very cheap date.
2. Her body fat is too low to allow menstruation—no periods, no birth control!
3. She's easily manipulated due to low self-esteem.
4. She looks about 13.

Disadvantages:
1. Never swallows.

....

Weight-Loss Vocabulary

Cow: Anyone else. Or yourself, if you eat. Examples: *She's such a cow.* Or, *I'm such a cow.*

Walrus: Cow with a moustache. Example: *Whoa. Walrus.*

Triple digits: A hundred pounds or more. Example: *I'm pushing triple digits—can you say bovine?*

Squared: Snide *sotto voce* aside when someone underestimates their size. Example: *They say, "I'm a size 4," and under your breath you say, "squared," thus implying that they are actually closer to a size 16.*

BP: Abbreviation for "binge and purge." Example: *Jennifer and Jennifer and Lisa are totally having a BP party in Jennifer's room.*

Flipper: A woman so thin and lithe that she can be flipped around during coitus so as to resemble a young boy. Example: *Dude, she was a flipper.*

Sally (as in Struthers): Token fat woman that thin women keep around them so they will look even skinnier in comparison. Example: *Eat up, Sally.*

Pudding: Laxative-induced incontinence. Example: *Oh. My. God. Pudding.*

8.

The Ins and Outs of Self-Mutilation

Do You Need a Makeover?

1. Do you need a makeover?
   a. Yes
   b. No

SCORING THE QUIZ

If you answered "yes" to the above question, then you are already prepared to benefit from this chapter. Turn the page and start making positive changes!

If you answered "no" to the above question, then you are either Halle Berry or a liar. If you are Halle Berry, congratulations! You are fully sexy and have no need of a "mutilation makeover." Feel free to skip this chapter. As your career begins to decline, however, you should make sure to reread our chapters on alcohol and drug use.

If, on the other hand, you are not Halle Berry, it is important to understand the underlying reason for your mendacity.

It probably stems from societal messages telling you things like "be happy the way you are," or the ever-popular "if you love yourself, others will love you, too." It is understandable that you want to believe the advice of parents, teachers, and low-budget after-school specials, but honestly, if you jumped off a bridge, would other people jump just because you did? Of course they wouldn't, and they will not love you just because you do, either. In fact, if you dwell on it for a few long moments, you will realize the chances are fairly high that no one will ever love you. What you can realistically hope for, though, is to get a little attention, and that is ultimately what self-mutilation is all about: getting people to pay attention to you. Are you ready to give it a try?

The Mutilation Makeover

What is wrong with this picture? If you are thinking "nothing," you are entirely correct. Slim, well-proportioned, and generally considered "pretty" by family and friends, Donna is physically flawless, and therein lies her problem. She exudes none of the self-loathing that men find so attractive in women. There is nothing degrading or disgusting about her appearance, nothing to suggest inner demons, low self-esteem, and/or a desperate desire to be noticed that's so all-consuming it swallows all chastity, morality, and moderation. Donna, in short, needs a mutilation makeover—a few hints of "bad girl" to accent and undermine her "good girl" image. At the end of this chapter you will see what

Donna

our makeover experts were able to do for Donna, and also for the previously pedestrian Dave.

Of course, Donna and Dave are just examples. The real question is, what kind of self-mutilation is right for you? Could a simple tattoo make the difference between getting that promotion and getting passed over? Or might you require breast or penis enlargement in order to build self-confidence and enhance your social cachet? Or perhaps even a slightly more intense form of ritual scarification? Whatever you decide, we are here to help. With the guidance of self-anointed experts and unpaid interns, we have catalogued and analyzed a wide variety of self-mutilation looks, ranging from the **popular** to the **plastic** to the **profound.** Feel free to experiment with various styles, even mixing and matching them to suit your taste. It is, after all, your body. Let your imagination run free!

Dave

The Popular

Piercing

Smooth, unblemished skin connotes good health, good hygiene, and good morals. You can go a long way toward avoiding such "wholesome" stereotypes by puncturing the skin of both face and body with crudely fashioned metallic objects. Facial and body piercings indicate to others that you have a wild or "freaky" side, and that you are willing to undergo mild discomfort in your quest for uniqueness.

THE QUEST FOR INDIVIDUALITY Piercing is about setting yourself apart from the crowd and being your own person, especially when you are confined in an institutional setting such as high school or college. If you go to a small school, there is still a good chance that you can be one of the first ten or fifteen people in your immediate peer group to indicate your individuality with an eyebrow or nose ring. It is important, though, that you act quickly. Think how embarrassing it would be to be the only person in your school not expressing your antiestablishment uniqueness through piercing!

 DID YOU KNOW? *"NEZ PERCE" IS NATIVE AMERICAN FOR "IRK PARENTS."*

THE SECRET EARRING CODE If you are a man considering earrings, it is essential to know the secret earring code. A single earring in your right ear indicates that you are **openly gay.** A single earring in your left ear indicates that you are **latently gay.** Multiple earrings in any ear indicate that you have **poor taste.**

THE SELF-DESTRUCTION HANDBOOK

PIERCING HISTORY The practice of piercing goes back more than 5,000 years. Roman men pierced their nipples in order to indicate courage, while Egyptian royalty pierced their genitals to indicate strength and virility. The earliest known evidence of piercing comes from a set of cave drawings discovered in ancient Mesopotamia, and reproduced here.

Tattoos

Tattoos have become a definite fashion trend, and at this point it is virtually impossible for women to get admitted to certain clubs in LA and New York without a serpentine tattoo on their lower back, peeking out just above a pair of low-rise jeans. One of the most unique and interesting things about tattoos is that they showcase your willingness to make a major commitment on the spur of the moment.

COMMITTING TO THE TREND Unlike bell-bottoms, Mohawks, and other fashion fads, tattoos are permanent. Even 15 years from now, when tattoos have gone the way of feathered hair and Members Only jackets, your homage to this ephemeral trend will be forever etched on your person. In a sense, having a permanent tattoo is not unlike having Dexy's Midnight Runners playing continuously on your stereo forever. How cool is that?

A TATTOO MAKEOVER STORY Natalie spent most of her life taking the "safe" route. She grew up in the suburbs, married her college sweetheart, and had two lovely children with him, but she always felt there was a little something missing. Fortunately, last year she turned to us for help, and our makeover expert suggested that she accent her homemaker image with a tattoo. Natalie agreed, and after a careful selection process they chose a pictograph of the Chinese word for "skank," located on her lower back just above the tailbone. It came out beautifully:

Natalie: "I never would have believed a single tattoo could have such a profound effect on my life, but it has. I hardly ever used to go out partying or anything, but now my girlfriends and I go out all the time. We wear tight belly-shirts and low-rise pants and walk right to the front of lines at clubs and the bouncer waves us in like we're stars or something. Men buy us drinks the whole night, and never once have I had to call a cab to get a ride home—there are always lots of offers from guys with really hot cars and Jacuzzis. It's just so cool. It's the way college should have been."

Natalie's Husband: "One neat thing is that I get a lot more quality time alone with the kids now that Natalie's out so much with her friends. I think the kids used to take their mom a little bit for granted—heck, we all did—but now they're just so happy to see her whenever she comes home. And this tattoo has done wonders for Natalie's self-confidence—especially in the boudoir, if you'll pardon my French. Since she got the tattoo it's almost as though she's had a team of specialists working around the clock to tutor her in every conceivable way of pleasing a man. Let me tell you, if I'd known a tattoo could do all that, I'd have gotten her one a long time ago."

Colorful Hair Dye

While not particularly interesting or attractive, bold hair colors such as pink, blue, or green do an excellent job of announcing "I'm thirteen and have overindulgent parents."

DID YOU KNOW? LAST YEAR, THE KAPPA KAPPA SIGMA GIRLS WHO WENT TO CABO FOR SPRING BREAK ALL GOT BUTTERFLY TATTOOS ON THEIR LEFT ANKLES EXCEPT FOR JENNIFER SAVERI, BUT SHE HARDLY EVEN COUNTS AS A KAPPA SIG ANYMORE BECAUSE SHE'S BASICALLY ALWAYS EITHER STUDYING OR HANGING OUT WITH HER BOYFRIEND.

WHAT DOES YOUR TATTOO SAY ABOUT YOU?

A NUDE WOMAN Tattooing a nude woman on your arm indicates that you are a true connoisseur of the female form. It suggests a deep and abiding respect for the fair sex that thinking women will immediately recognize and respond to.

CHINESE CHARACTERS Chinese characters are always cool because they indicate your cosmopolitanism: You are down with ancient cultures, even if you don't have the slightest idea where to find them on a map.

YOUR OWN NAME Sometimes you simply want to indicate abject stupidity and a total lack of imagination. In this case, tattooing yourself with your own name or initials is just the ticket.

FACTS ABOUT THE PERSON YOU ARE SWORN TO KILL If you have lost your long-term memory but retain a vague sense that you need to track down and kill someone, a very cool and cinematically effective way to facilitate this quest is to tattoo reminders about that person all over your body.

The Plastic

Breast Implants

Breast augmentation is the fastest-growing form of plastic surgery, and for good reason. Women are finally beginning to understand the inherent attractiveness of heretofore natural skin stretched to painful extremes by artificially implanted bags of fluid. There are still some women who seek "natural-looking" implants, but remember, it's called *plastic* surgery, not *natural* surgery. Breast implants are your way of communicating a willingness to sacrifice money, comfort, and basic health in order to please the opposite sex.

In addition to exciting men sexually, cripplingly large breasts also put them at ease emotionally—proving that you have no intention of engaging in any non-sexual activities such as sports, work, or running away. If you do feel the need to retain some mobility, a good compromise is stripper-style spherical implants, which make for less egregiously large but still obviously faux breasts. Men are irresistibly drawn to these gravity-defying globes, perhaps because they are so ill-fitted to a woman's body that they seem almost detachable, as if a man could simply remove and carry them away.

REASONS FOR BREAST-ENHANCEMENT SURGERY

1. Breasts are small, mannish
2. Because you never get a second chance to make a desperately overemphatic first impression
3. You would like your fair chance at landing Kid Rock
4. Knowledge that your ex-boyfriend will see them, covet them, but never, ever, as long as he lives, touch them
5. Your wealthy "uncle" wishes it

Penis Enlargement

It is difficult to compare genital size while flaccid, so the best way to determine if you need a penis enlargement is to **rent a pornographic video.** Are you as large as the men in the film? Do women **moan and writhe** like that when you have intercourse with them? If not, you are probably a good candidate for penis-enlargement surgery.

HOW BIG IS TOO BIG? Conventional wisdom says that you cannot be too big. It is important to remember, however, that penile additions are essentially "dead weight," that each centimeter you add decreases your ability to feel anything other than a dull ache during sex, and that you'll have the pleasure of experiencing a pain like passing a kidney stone every time you urinate. While such side effects are a small price to pay for the appearance of virility, it may nonetheless be wise for those in monogamous relationships to combine a more moderate enlargement for him with some form of vaginal rejuvenation for her (see below).

REASONS FOR PENIS-ENLARGEMENT SURGERY

1. Asian
2. Nagging feeling that penis should be reflective of ego
3. Tired of seeing a single tear slide down the cheek of your girlfriend whenever she prepares to fellate you
4. Because everyone in the shower at the gym really will think more of you
5. Your wealthy "uncle" wishes it

GLUTEUS MINIMUS?

Across the nation, many young Caucasian women are listening to rap music and shaking their . . . Well, the truth is they are not shaking much. But that can change! With new buttock enhancement technology, there is no reason anyone needs to go through life "half-assed." A 30-minute outpatient surgery can give even the slenderest, waspiest women "urban" asses of their very own. If you are unsure about what an "urban" ass can do for you, ask yourself one question: Does J.Lo have a multimillion-dollar career because she can act or sing?

Vaginal Rejuvenation

Are you tired of that wrinkled, loose flesh in and around your vagina? Doctors can surgically reshape your pubic area to give it a smoother, more youthful appearance. Furthermore, they can also tighten the interior to such an extent that every encounter with your partner will feel like "the first time"— exquisite friction and sense of conquest for him, burning pain and mild to moderate bleeding for you.

Calf Implants

The fastest-growing form of implant surgery among men is calf implants, and the reason for this is simple: sex appeal. Money, looks, and power are still important, but few things turn a woman on more reliably than oversized calves.

Lip Augmentation

For reasons not yet entirely understood, men are irresistibly drawn to the possibility of violent things happening in and around a woman's mouth. With a few outpatient collagen injections, you can achieve the "fat lip" look that is currently so popular with supermodels, C-list actresses, and victims of domestic violence.

The Pout

The Porn Star

The Elvis

The Profound

Scars

Scars are sexy because there is always a story behind them—they're like an open invitation to personal conversation, a hint of mystery and danger marked forever on the skin. If you are a man with little else to recommend him, **lying about your scars** can be a powerful way of impressing a woman.

SENSE OF SENSIBILITY The most common mistake men make when lying about their scars is fabricating a story that would impress other men. Women do not care about knife-fighting or rock-climbing injuries, or anything else that results from acts of physical daring. They are more attuned to emotional trauma, and you should make sure that your scar story has plenty of pathos behind it. You might assert, for example, that you got your scar while trying to save your little brother from the fire, but you were too small and couldn't reach him—you lost him that day and you lost part of yourself, too, a part that haunts you when you hear his laugh in yours, stealing your breath like a ghost and forever mixing grief with your mirth.

LESS IS MORE The only problem with falsehoods like the one above is that they involve statements that can be disproved. This is not an issue if you are simply going for a one-night relationship, but in the long run the best scar lies are ones that do not make statements of fact. The idea is to say little or nothing overtly, instead letting her fill in the emotional blanks. If a woman asks you where a given scar came from, for example, try allowing a faraway look to come into your eyes, and say, "It's not something I can talk about." This gives an impression of pain and depth of character. She will imagine herself healing your psychic wounds and believe that sometime in the future, as tears fill your eyes and the background music winnows to a single Yanni-like note of prolonged pathos, you will confess to her your darkest secret and she will become bound to you as lover and confessor, the protector of your psyche, the keeper of your soul. Equally important, you will not have said anything she can later disprove and use against you when the relationship turns ugly.

Cutting

Cutting is a fast-growing form of female self-mutilation that is satisfying, inexpensive, and easy to do at home. The only accoutrements you will need are a cutting implement and some sort of obsessive-compulsive disorder.

CUTTING ME SOFTLY The sexy thing about cutting is that it is at once **self-mutilative and subtle.** Far from the overly flamboyant, pink-hair-and-nose-ring types, cutters tend to be dark, closeted, diffident, and pale. Their hidden scars are like keys to a secret underworld of masochistic fervor and violent self-abnegation, a purgatorial place where conventional morality means nothing and only dullness is feared.

WHERE TO CUT? While fingers, feet, and inner thighs are all acceptable locations, the **forearm** remains the canvas of choice for dedicated cutters. It offers a wide and easily accessible expanse of unmarked flesh, a veritable Alaskan Wildlife Preserve just waiting to be despoiled by unsanctioned drilling.
Forearms also have a long and distinguished legacy of **sui-**

cide **"attempts,"** and the overall sexiness of forearm cuts, and indeed of cutting in general, is at least partially derived from this association with the ultimate self-destructive behavior. Anyone can claim that they're "really depressed" or that their therapist put them on a "suicide watch," but most of them are just posing. When accompanied by a dusky demeanor and a sound track of early Morrissey, however, a light network of scars on the wrists and forearms can lend real legitimacy to your existential complaints and help give you the "suicide advantage."

The Suicide Advantage

Taking your suicidal thoughts public has long been a way of announcing "depth" and revealing your "dark side." Whether you are a man or a woman, suicidal tendencies make you extremely attractive to members of the opposite sex. For women, "suicidal" tendencies indicate to men that you have low self-esteem and a "nothing to lose" sensibility, thus suggesting that you will be easily manipulated and open to most forms of depravity. For men, your "suicidal" impulses suggest to women that you are deep, artistic, and likely to start a band.

"SUICIDE" TECHNIQUE: DON'T OVERDO IT The most important thing to remember when staging a suicide "attempt" is that **you do not really want to die.** Devices such as guns, nooses, and large motorized vehicles should be avoided, because they are far too dangerous both to yourself and to others.

Wrist-cutting is an excellent choice for a suicide "attempt" because the damage is easily controlled, yet makes a powerful statement. Some people, however, simply do not like blood.

In this case, the next most reliable form of faux suicide remains the **drug "overdose."**

STAGING YOUR "OVERDOSE" When staging an "overdose," pick a comfortable spot on a floor or bed to lie down on, then sprinkle a few pills nearby. Place the open pill bottle haphazardly on its side, as though dropped there. A nice accent to this look is a half-empty bottle of hard liquor. Even if you don't drink, you can still purchase the bottle and pour some of it down the sink. Allowing what remains in the bottle to drop from your hand and spill lavishly on the floor can greatly enhance the overall effect of your "OD," but be sure to remember: You're not actually going to die, so there will be cleanup to consider!

A SCENT OF SUICIDE

Those who want to capture the ethos of self-annihilation without risk of physical harm may wish to try *Suicide*—a haunting and dangerous new fragrance from Calvin Klein.

The "After" Pictures

Donna

Dave

Conclusion

*C*ONGRATULATIONS! By reading this book, you have begun an exciting journey into a world of debauchery, delinquency, and self-degradation. Even if you lack the courage and imagination to take any of our advice, remember that you have still wasted a good deal of time reading it—time that might otherwise have been used to accomplish something constructive. That's right, procrastination is itself a legitimate self-destructive behavior, and the fact that you are reading this now means that you have already started down a delightfully slippery slope toward a more despicable existence. It is, as they say, all downhill from here!

Now that you have completed the book, you may have concerns about whether you will be able to maintain your chosen self-destructive behaviors on your own. Well, the good news is, you don't have to! That's right, as far as we're concerned, you are now a full-fledged member of the Self-Hurt family, and if you ever feel the need for advice on, say, maintaining a long-term adulterous relationship, or you just want support from a like-minded community of self-destructives, you will find it on our chatboard at www.selfdestructionhandbook.com. Once

again, that's www.selfdestructionhandbook.com. So go ahead—
drink up, light up, shoot up, and screw up. In short, enjoy
yourself, and know that we will always be there to help you
not help yourself.

About the Authors

ADAM WASSON is a Scotch-swilling, relationship-sabotaging, Marlboro-smoking MWM. He enjoys walks on the beach, sodomitical literature, and good food. He is looking for: a small but vehement cult following.
• •

JESSICA STAMEN is an SWF with a kind heart, question-able morals, and a history of Oprahesque weight fluctuation. She is looking for: a man.
• •